What others are saying about Jeff Smith and
STRESS-FREE SUCCESS

Stress-Free Success will take its place among the best-selling books of recent times. A plethora of easy-to-understand concepts and ideas will help even the most skeptical reader live a happier, more successful life." **John Assaraf**, *CEO, Planet City*

"*Stress-Free Success* had me hooked from the beginning! Jeff Smith's warm writing style encouraged me to complete the exercises from start to finish. I found myself continually marveling at the book's magnificent simplicity. For perhaps the first time I became aware of how to evaluate where I am in my life, set goals for my future and coordinate a timetable for making those goals happen."
Beth Wilson, *owner, Write For You*

"Jeff Smith is not only a serious student of human potential, he is a master of in-depth research. This book is loaded with factual information that will help anyone improve the quality of their life."
Bob Proctor, *author, international best-seller, You Were Born Rich*

"This guy is on to something! Jeff Smith's *Stress-Free Success* is a profound yet simple approach to something all of us are looking for. Setting and achieving goals, using affirmations and visualization to habitually focus on what you want is easy, fun and powerfully productive. This is information from the great masters rolled into a user-friendly book." **Mark Meyerdirk**, *CEO, LifeSuccess Institute*

"Every once in a while we come across people who aren't just interested but are committed to designing the life they desire. Jeff is a true student of this process and has decided to lay out the rules of this game called life. I've learned much about focus and success from this man and I'm glad to see he's sharing his gifts with the rest of the world. My suggestion to readers is to not only READ this information, but LEARN it, LIVE it, and SHARE it."
Jim Bunch, *co-creator of Are You Programmed For Success Or Failure?*

"This book is totally innovative from beginning to end! You will experience an in-depth personal expedition that will reveal an inner self you never knew existed. This book will prove to be an intricate part of your new personal development." **Lynn Rank**, *Service Business & Management Consultant*

"Many motivational books leave us excited, but frustrated; you know there's more, but you don't know how to access it. *Stress-Free Success* solves that problem perfectly. In it, Jeff outlines the process one step at a time and substantiates each point with recognized research. In the book, you'll gain all kinds of insight into your own feelings and thought processes. Then, you'll be given <u>painless, yet exciting, ways to change any result you'd like to change in your life</u>. I started out with a hodgepodge of values, ideas, expectations, and misgivings.

I completed the book knowing a whole lot more about myself, believing in myself, <u>feeling in control</u>, and ready to challenge myself."
Karin Henderson, *president, Home Support Services, Inc.*

"*Stress-Free Success* is a <u>goldmine of information for anyone really serious about improving their life and cutting stress out</u>. It's a complete 'how-to' manual on being successful, reaching your goals and living life to the fullest without stress. It CAN be done, and Jeff reveals how in this unique and inspirational book." **Mike Fry**, *president, Fancy Fortune Cookies*

"In *Stress-Free Success*, Jeff Smith has captured in a simple way the road to success. A must for anyone who truly desires success while at the same time <u>balancing a healthy spiritual and personal life</u>."
Michele Blood, *author of Affirmation Power and co-creator of Musivations programs*

"What made *Stress-Free Success* different for me was that I had so much FUN reading it! While reading Jeff's book, <u>I felt like a kid making a Christmas wish list all over again - except this time I KNEW I really could have everything I wished for</u>! And, *Stress-Free Success* not only taught me how to grow as an individual, it <u>also showed me how to empower my 3rd grade students</u> with their own goals and dreams about their futures. This is truly a book for ALL ages!" **Shelley Stuteville**, *3rd grade teacher*

"*Stress-Free Success* will satisfy your quest for the answers you need to be successful and to enjoy your success once you've achieved it. The way in which Jeff presents the information is brilliant - very easy to read and understand. <u>You, too, can enjoy all life has to offer. Just read the book and put into action the ideas within. Keep the book close by. You'll want to reference it time and time again, as I have done</u>."
Murray Smith, *executive vice president, WWW.Planet City.Com*

Stress-Free SUCCESS

How To Really Achieve
All Your Goals
<u>Without</u> Giving Up
Your Life

Jeffrey D. Smith

CENTER FOR PERSONAL EXCELLENCE

STRESS-FREE SUCCESS
©1997 by Jeffrey D. Smith

All rights reserve. No part of this book may be reproduced or transmitted in any form or by any means, electronic or mechanical, including photocopying, recording, or by any information storage or retrieval system, without written permission from the author, Jeffrey D. Smith, except for the inclusion of quotations in a review. For information address Jeffrey D. Smith, c/o Center For Personal Excellence, 3156 Woodview Ridge, Suite 301, Kansas City, KS 66103.

This book may be purchased for educational, business, or sales promotional use. For information, please write to Special Markets Dept. at the address above.

Printed in the United States of America. Inside pages printed by Corporate Document Services, Kansas City, ph: 913-384-0066. Cover printed by Quality Litho, Kansas City, ph: 913-262-5341.

FIRST EDITION

ISBN 1-890190-19-5

How to order

Single copies may be ordered from The Center For Personal Excellence; telephone (888) 533-3764. Quantity discounts are also available.

Dedication

To my Grandmother Rupp,
*You're no longer with us in body,
but you'll always be with me in Spirit.
Thanks for all the love we share.*

Acknowledgments

Stress-Free Success is truly a collaboration among the many people who have had an impact on my life and my achievements. I'd like to acknowledge those that made this book possible:

My mother, Alyce,
for teaching me the meaning of unconditional love

Norma,
for loving me and being such a special part of our family

My brother, Tod, and his wife, Jeni
for being the best brother and sister-in-law I could ever ask for

My father David, his wife Dorothy, and my grandparents
for being a wonderful family to me

John Assaraf and Murray Smith
for your support, friendship, and encouragement

Mark Victor Hansen
for being an example of life's most wonderful qualities

Kim Crosby, Beth Wilson, Mark Meyerdirk, Bob Proctor, and the rest of the associates and staff at the LifeSuccess Institute

Ann Price-Perkins, the rest of my Indianapolis Mastermind Group, my baseball coaches, writing advisers, and the many other friends, authors, entrepreneurs and teachers who I've learned from and who have encouraged me through the years

And last, but certainly not least, to my two best friends,

My Success Partner, Mike Fry
You are a true *friend and I'm looking forward to sharing thousands more successes with each other!*

and Shelley Stuteville,
*for your enthusiasm, support, friendship and love.
You truly are an angel!*

Many thanks to all of you for helping me grow into the person that I am today and for helping me learn to open up and share my gifts with others.

What you will learn in this book..

Lesson 1: The Fundamentals of the Stress-Free Success System

What is stress? What is success? How can you achieve Stress-Free Success? The Myth of Self-Improvement; The 4 Keys to Stress-Free Success

Lesson 2: Figure Out Where You're Starting From

Determine where you are now in each area of your life

Lesson 3: The Y Factor - Why You Are Where You Are

The Y Factor explains WHY you are where you are; how the three parts of your nature work together to create the results you get in your life; how to change any result in your life; why most "positive thinking" doesn't work; how to overcome bad habits and negative conditioning

Lesson 4: Decide Where You Want To Be

Why what happened in the past is irrelevant to today and tomorrow; The Principle Of The Blank Page; how Psycho-Cybernetics control your life - and how to use them to make success easy and automatic; how to create "Your Million-Dollar Image; what kind of person will you become?; building your Dream Book; creating Your Ideal Day and Your Ideal Lifestyle

Lesson 5: Develop A Solid Foundation For Achieving Your Goals

Your Life's Focus; why you need a focus or mission statement and what benefits it gives you; what role does destiny play in your life?; what are you willing to dedicate your life to?; how to create your Focus or Mission Statement; The Power Of Giving and why it's critical to your success; create your Personal Creed;

how your Personal Creed eliminates stress from your life and makes decision-making easy; Napoleon Hill's and John Wooden's Personal Creeds; the only way to grow; how to break out of your comfort zone; 3 killers of success and happiness to avoid.

Lesson 6: Adopt A Stress-Free Belief System

How to determine if your current beliefs are adding or removing stress from your life; the 4 keys to a Stress-Free Belief System; the TRUE meaning of wealth; does everything happen for a reason?; the importance of not attaching labels to things; Direct Alternatives vs. Indirect Alternatives - how to keep control of your life without feeling stressed; Using The Secret of Stress-Free Success;

Lesson 7: Eliminate The Stress-Causing Beliefs You Now Hold

The power of paradigms; how to make huge improvements quickly; why "common sense" will get you in trouble; lies we believe; the best way to develop quality relationships; why poverty is not a virtue; what prejudice REALLY means and why 93% of Americans are prejudiced; why you have trouble letting go of the past and what to do about it; how to avoid one of the biggest wastes of your time;

The 5 Biggest Lies About Your Happiness that you probably believe; why other people do NOT make you happy; the ONLY cause of unhappiness and how to avoid it; why suffering today to enjoy something tomorrow is wrong; why suffering does NOT make you a more noble, pure person; how to quit suffering once and for all

The surprising reason you aren't as wealthy as you could be today; what almost no one understands about money; The 7 Biggest Lies You Believe About Money; why you don't NEED money; why it doesn't always take money to make money; creating wealth even if you're not particularly smart; the biggest Biblical mistake about money; why money WON'T solve your problems; the true source of all your problems.

Lesson 8: Harness GOAL POWER To Multiply Your Success Without Stress

The sad truth about goals; why are goals important?; the true purpose of goals

Lesson 9: Use The 20 Laws Of Stress-Free "Goal-Getting"

The Ultimate Scorecard; why you don't have to know HOW you're going to achieve your goal; the only reason you don't already have your goal; the Law of Cause & Effect; why it takes no more effort to succeed than it does to fail; your mind cannot function on the opposite of an idea; how to get rid of the ties that hold you back; what winners focus on; why there are no true barriers in our lives; you have no proof that you can't achieve your goals; why WHAT you do is more important than HOW you do it; the 5 Laws of Mind; how to compound your success quickly without working any harder; why you should leave the urgent things for later; why you should forget about time management - and how this "forgetfulness" will CUT DOWN the time it takes to achieve your goals; how the Goal Achievement Process works; the stress-free way to stay focused 100% of the time.

Lesson 10: The Power Of Dream-Building - Defining Your Ideal Stress-Free Life

How to decide what you want out of life; the 3-step process for defining your ideal stress-free life; questions to ask yourself to help you clarify what you really want; the Success System that never works - what NOT to do; goals NOT to choose; reaching for your Big Ultimate Dream; the 3-part acid test for your Big Ultimate Dream;

Lesson 11: Turn Your Dreams Into Achievable Goals

The 4-step process for achieving your goals; the keys to transforming your dreams into reality; checklist for evaluating your Primary Overall Goal

Lesson 12: Develop An Effective Stress-Free Success Plan

The 7 steps to develop an effective Stress-Free Success Plan; how to let go of the past; Frank Sinatra doesn't move pianos; how to eliminate distractions without feeling stressed; how to simplify your life; how to eliminate your fears; how to decide what to do each day to achieve your goals; what is the first step toward achieving your goal?; the 12 keys for making time your ally;

Your Daily Half Dozen and how they move you smoothly toward your goals without stress; the 3 steps of executing your Stress-Free Success Plan; the critical role of belief and desire in achieving your goals; the one thing you can doubt without affecting the achievement of your goals; why you must get emotionally involved in your goal BEFORE you will ever achieve it; how to build desire for your goal; how to check your progress; the best way to reward yourself for your successes

Lesson 13: Execute Your Success Plan & Enjoy The Results

The simple method for executing your Stress-Free Success Plan; how to use "flow" to experience joy in every moment of your life; the 7-step formula for enjoying all the activities in your life; your very own Gold Mind; use the "Secret Of The Razor's Edge" to become a Stress-Free Champion in record time

Lesson 14: Your Next Step - Work With A SuccessCoach Who Can Help You Stay On Track To Stress-Free Success

Why a coach is important to your success; how a coach can help you; how to choose a coach; where to find the best coach

Preface

> *"When one sees eternity in things that pass away and infinity in finite things, then one has pure knowledge."* **Bhagavad Gita**

The book you have in your hands may be the most important book you'll ever read. In its pages, you'll find the Stress-Free Success System, a system that has been designed to help you **shatter the myth that success is hard or stressful** and break through this false belief system into a world of happiness, joy, peace, and love.

Although this book does offer a step-by-step system for achieving Stress-Free Success, I do not intend for this to be a book of "insider tips on how to be happy and successful." Each of our lives is uniquely our own. We are all different. We can create our ideal life in our own way.

There is no standard recipe to follow.

There are, however, timeless principles that we can learn that will make our journey much more natural and enjoyable.

That's what this book is intended to share - the Principles of Stress-Free Success that you can apply in your own unique way to create the life that you would like to live.

> *There is no promise of shortcuts in these pages, but there is a concrete plan that if followed will lead you straight down the path to your ideal life.*

All I can do with this book is offer you a coherent method of examining your own life, determining what is working and what needs improving, and then outlining a plan to do more of what works and less of what doesn't work. This is a process of insight into *your own* nature.

Lesson 1:
Learn The Fundamentals Of The Stress-Free Success System

Is it possible to achieve Stress-Free Success?
The title of this book makes a bold promise.

Right now, you're wondering if you can achieve what the title of this book promises - or if it's just a bunch of "hot air", like so many other so-called "success" books.

Well, I'm here to tell you, **it is possible to achieve Stress-Free Success** - *if* we understand what that really means.

So let's start with that: getting a clear picture of what Stress-Free Success *really* means.

Quick- tell me what success means to you.

If you're like most people, you had trouble answering that question in specific terms. You probably got a picture in your mind of a beautiful new house, shiny sports car, or sun-drenched beach. You may have thought of your family gathered around the dinner table with smiles on their faces. Or a large paycheck being sent to you on a regular basis.

Those all could be components of success, but they don't really define success. And, without getting a clear definition of success, it'll be kind of hard to determine when we achieve it, don't you think?

So let's address that question again:

What does success *really* mean?
Robert Louis Stevenson said,

> *"That man (or woman) is a success who has lived well, laughed often and loved much; who has gained the respect of intelligent men (and*

women) and the love of children; who has filled his niche and accomplished his task; who leaves the world better than he found it, whether by an improved poppy, a perfect poem or a rescued soul; who never lacked appreciation of earth's beauty or failed to express it; who looked for the best in others and gave the best he had."
(parens added)

Bob Dylan summed it up simply,

"A man is a success if he gets up in the morning and goes to bed at night and in between does what he wants to do."

And, **Earl Nightingale** offered one of the most famous definitions of success:

"Success is the progressive realization of a worthy ideal."

If you study each of those definitions, you'll begin to get a pretty clear picture of what success really is.

As you can see, none of these writers said success is lots of money or luxury cars or new homes. All these things are symbols of success, but they are not true success.

Objects and experiences such as these exist on the physical surface of our world. Success, however, is much deeper than that.

As William H. Danforth said,

"Our most valuable possessions are those which can be shared without lessening; those which, when shared, multiply. Our least valuable possessions are those which, when divided, are diminished."

Read that quote again. It contains a key distinction in the concept of success.

"Our most valuable possessions are those which can be shared without lessening; those which, when

shared, multiply. Our least valuable possessions are those which, when divided, are diminished."

That means that money and all the things it buys are one of the LEAST valuable possessions we have. Yet most of us spend the majority of our lives working at jobs we can't stand just to earn some money to buy some things that are some of the least valuable possessions in our entire lives.

That makes just about no sense at all.

Yet almost everyone does it.

Why?

Because they think they have to. Or because they feel it's the right thing to do because everyone else is doing it. Or because they think there is no other way.

Well, I'm here to tell you, **that's stupid.** You CAN be different. You don't HAVE to do this. It isn't the RIGHT thing to do just because everyone else is doing it. And there IS another way.

And that way is what you will learn in this book- the path that allows you to achieve **TRUE SUCCESS, "The ability to fulfill your heart's true desires with effortless ease while you live in harmony with the world around you."**

You'll be able to drive your dream car, live in your dream home, and go on luxurious vacations around the world. But you'll realize that the true value in these things comes not from the things themselves, but from the wisdom and understanding that you must develop in order to earn them and from the love they allow you to share when you possess them.

The wisdom, understanding, and love are the possessions that "when shared, multiply." They are the essence of true success.

The question you probably now have is, "Okay, Jeff, I've got a pretty good understanding of what success really means, but doesn't it take tons of hard work, blood, sweat, and tears to ever achieve that level of success where I can make all my dreams come true? How can I ever do it without feeling stressed out all the time?"

Let me just tell you this.

There is a way.

A way to achieve all your goals without feeling stressed. And that's what you'll learn in the rest of this book. But before we get to that, we need to get a clear picture of what Stress really is so we understand what it is we're really trying to eliminate from our lives.

What does Stress-Free really mean?

When most people think of stress, they think of those feelings of tension they get when their lives feel out of control, when they feel overwhelmed with all there is to do, or when they feel fear about doing something they're not sure they can do.

This is unnecessary stress and it's completely avoidable. Here's why:

Open your mind for a minute and ask yourself this,

What are we referring to when we speak of "ourself"? What is "our self" really?

The answer to that is rather simple, if you think about it for a minute.

"Our Self" consists of three main parts - what we can see, what we can't see, and the link between the two. That translates into our physical body (what we can see), our universal or spiritual side (what we can't see), and our intellectual nature (the bridge between the two).

Our <u>physical body</u> and the world it lives in is a representation of our beliefs, thoughts, and other mental patterns.

Our <u>universal nature</u> is our "ideal of perfection." It is the part of us that represents all that is good.

Stress-Free Success • 12

Our <u>intellectual nature</u> is kind of like the controls on our television set. It determines which channel we're going to tune into and how focused the picture on that channel will be. We can tune in to our physical world channel, our universal/spiritual channel, or a channel in between.

At some points in our life, it is more appropriate to tune in to the physical channel. At other times, it is more appropriate to tune in to the universal channel. And, at other points, we should be tuned in to the "combo" channels in between.

How do we know which channel to tune in to at which time? That is what you will learn in this book. Basically, though, the way to determine the proper channel to tune in to is to learn to listen to the messages your body, mind, and soul are giving you and then learn to fine-tune your channel selection to be in harmony with these messages.

Thinking in these terms, we can define stress very simply and very accurately:

Stress is the static that occurs when we are not tuned in to the proper channel at the proper time.

In other words, **stress occurs when our body, mind, and soul are out of balance. It is a conflict between "our head and our heart"** - when our heart is telling us one thing and our head another.

When we're tuned to a channel that doesn't pick up the proper amount of nourishment for our body, mind, and soul, we get "static". We feel this "static" as stress.

This type of stress is unnecessary and eliminatable. You see, in our deepest, most fundamental core, we are all spiritual beings having a human existence. On this spiritual level, we have the wisdom that allows to always be "on the right channel" to allow our lives to be full of happiness, peace, joy, and bliss.

It is our responsibility as human beings to continually improve our ability to choose the "proper channel" for our lives. The better we get at choosing this channel, the more stress just melts gently out of our lives, like a pat of butter in the sun.

Then, one day, we'll find that all the unnecessary stress has completely melted out of our life and we'll be left with pure joy and love for ourselves and everyone and everything around us.

The 4 Keys To Stress-Free Success

Now that you understand what Stress-Free Success really means, you are ready to begin using The 3 Keys To Success. Here are the four keys:

1. *Figure out where you are now*
2. *Decide where you want to go*
3. *Understand how you got your present results and how to get new ones*
4. *Use this understanding to put together and execute a plan to get to where you want to go*

That's it, you say?

I know, it sounds far too simple to actually work, but its simplicity is why it does work. <u>Too many of us needlessly complicate our lives with all kinds of personal development gobblydegook that does more to confuse us than help us.</u> This simple formula has created thousands of millionaires, been the key to countless loving relationships, and has helped untold numbers of people around the world live dreams they never thought were possible. It'll do the same for you - IF you follow each step.

> *You see, the Keys To Success are like the steps in building a house. If you don't build the foundation or decide to only put up three walls, you're not going to have much of a house when you're done.*

Every step is important and you can't skip steps if you want the end result to be exactly the way you want it to be. That said, let's move on to the first step...

Lesson 2:
Figure Out Where You're Starting From

Where are you now?

The first thing you need to understand before you can go about changing the results you're getting in your life is where you are today.

> *Imagine yourself waking up one morning and saying, "Gee, I'd really like to visit Dallas today." Without knowing where you are starting from, you obviously would have no clue which direction to start going to reach Dallas. If you were lucky, you'd pick the right direction and get there. More than likely, though, even if you were totally determined to get to Dallas, you'd spend the better part of the rest of your life wandering around trying to figure out where Dallas is and how to get there.*

That's how most of us lead our lives - wandering around trying to get "somewhere" without really knowing where we're starting from or where we want to end up.

From this moment forward, promise yourself you won't fall into the "wandering" majority. You'll be different. You'll know where you're coming from and where you're going to.

And that'll make your journey more exciting and fun than anything you've ever experienced.

Let's begin by finding out exactly where you are today. Do a quick assessment of your situation.

Give yourself a score of 1 to 10 in the following areas: your income, your financial situation (assets, liabilities, retirement plan, etc), your career, your relationships, your health, your leisure activities, and your personal development or education.

Thinking about each of these areas of your life will give you a basic starting point for our next discussion.

Set up a worksheet like this to help you think through this exercise:

KEY LIFE AREA	WHERE I AM	WHERE I'D LIKE TO BE
Health		
Relationships		
Spirituality		
Social life		
Career		
Personal development		
Education		
Income		
Financial situation		

Look back at the worksheet you just created. Ask yourself these questions:

What areas of your life do you feel the most successful in?

What areas do you feel need the most work in?

What areas are the furthest from where you'd like to be a year from today?

What areas are the furthest from where you'd like to be 10 years from today?

Your answers to those questions give you a starting point for the exercises in the rest of this book. You now know, in general terms, where you are starting from. Once you know where you are starting from, you can decide where you want to go and figure out how to get there.

The key to this process is to first understand why you are where you are. Once you understand this, you will be able to change your results into exactly the ones that you want, permanently and effortlessly.

Lesson 3:
The Y Factor: Why You Are Where You Are & Why You CAN Achieve Any Goal You Choose

What is the Y Factor?

The next step in experiencing Stress-Free Success is to understand the Y Factor. **This is one of the most important parts of the book, so pay close attention** to this lesson. The Y Factor has three main parts:

1. Understand how *Y*ou work
2. Understand wh*Y* you are where you are
3. Understand how *Y*ou can change any result in your life

The Y Factor - Part I

How do we work?

To understand why you are where you are you first have to understand how your body and mind work. To illustrate this, we'll use the simple, but powerful Stickman diagram developed in 1934 by Dr. Thruman Fleet, a well-known chiropractor. I was introduced to this concept by Bob Proctor, author of *Born Rich*. Bob has effectively used this diagram in his seminars around the world for many years.

As you can see from the diagram on the next page, **each of us is made up of three parts: the universal (or spiritual), the intellectual, and the physical**.

You can view these three parts of your being like this:

1. What we see and can touch- the physical;
2. What we don't see and can't touch- the universal;
3. How the two are connected- the intellectual.

Our universal (spiritual) nature

The universal (or spiritual), part of our being corresponds to our subconscious mind full of non-physical thought-energy.

Our universal nature is like electricity. It is real power, even though you cannot see it or touch it. Just like electricity, it can be controlled and put to good or bad use, depending on your application of it. Imagine a powerful electric generator that you totally control. It is up to you whether to use it to power lights that illuminate the world or electric chairs that kill your fellow humans.

Our intellectual nature

The intellectual part of our nature corresponds to our conscious mind. This is where we do our thinking. It is the conference room where we decide what kind of device to hook our electrical generators up to. When we think, we are drawing power from the infinite voltage of Universal Intelligence. Since our power source is infinite, we are free to decide if we want to hook up a 15 watt bulb or 5000 watt bulb to our generator.

And, if we aren't getting the results we want in our lives, we can always pull out the bulb we're using and replace it with a new, more powerful one. This is how we break out of our ruts and create quantum changes in our lives.

The intellectual portion of our nature is made up of two parts: the **inductive** and the **deductive**. When you consciously choose your thoughts you are using the inductive portion of your nature. When thoughts unconsciously enter you, such as when you watch television, they enter through the deductive part of your nature.

Our physical nature

The third part of our nature is the physical. This corresponds to our body and the physical things in our world. In our analogy, this part of our nature would be the actual light that we have decided to hook our generator up to.

The Y Factor

The 3 Parts Of Our Being: How We Work

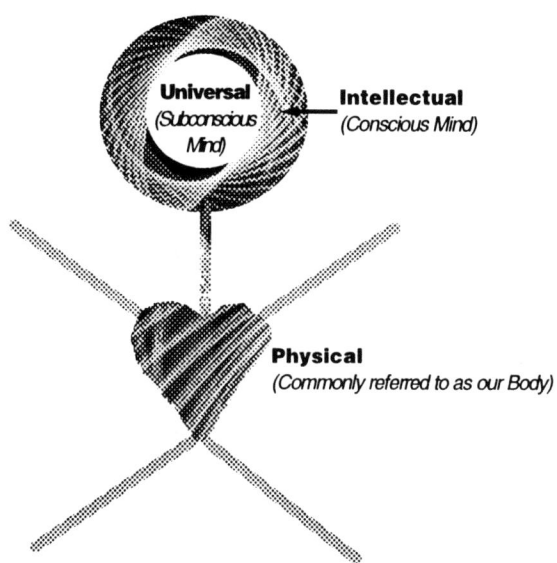

The 3 Parts Of Our Being

1. **Universal** = Subconscious Mind
The Universal part of our being is also called our subconscious mind. It is our connection to all other things in the Universe. It is here that Images form which trigger the emotions that we feel. These emotions lead to the actions that determine the results we get in our lives.

2. **Intellectual** = Conscious Mind
The Intellectual part of our being is also called our conscious mind. When we actively choose our thoughts, we can decide which images will form in our subconscious. Since these images control the results we get, this ability to choose our thoughts gives us control over the results in our lives.

When we passively allow thoughts to enter our mind, such as when we watch television, they pass directly into our subconscious mind, where images are formed that lead to new results in our life. Since most of the thoughts that enter our mind in this way are negative, this is one of the major reasons our results are often not what we want. We can prevent this from occurring by actively choosing thoughts that will lead to the results we want out fo life.

3. **Physical** = Body
The third portion of our being is our physical body. This is the instrument we use to take actions based upon the images in our subconscious mind.

The Y Factor - Part II

Wh**Y** you are where you are

The second part of the Y Factor is understanding how the universal, intellectual, and physical components of your nature work together to determine what results you are getting in your life. Here's how:

1. You consciously have **thoughts** (using your inductive nature) or unconsciously allow thoughts to enter your mind (through your deductive nature).

2. An **image** is formed of these thoughts and this image enters your subconscious mind, the universal portion of your nature.

   Your subconscious is totally deductive. It cannot reason or change the image so it accepts the exact image that is given to it. If enough similar images are placed into the subconscious, you will develop a belief or habit based on these images. This is called <u>conditioning</u> and is a major factor in determining how you look at yourself and the world around you, as well as what actions you take (or don't take) on a daily basis.

3. You then begin to have emotions and **feelings** based on the images that have been created in your subconscious mind. The strongest images (your strongest conditioning) will create the strongest emotions and feelings.

4. You then use your body, the physical portion of your nature, to take **action** based on the feelings you are having.

5. Finally, the actions that you take determine the **results** you get.

You can remember how this process works by thinking "T-I, FAR". Your "T"houghts create "I"mages which lead to "F"eelings that determine your "A"ctions which give you your "R"esults.

Work backwards through this process and you'll be able to easily understand **why you are where you are today**:

> 1. You have a certain set of present results.
> 2. Your present results are directly attributable to the actions you have taken.
> 3. These actions have depended on the emotions and feelings you were experiencing.
> 4. These emotions and feelings were caused by the images in your subconscious mind.
> 5. And, the images in your subconscious mind were formed by thoughts, which you either consciously chose or unconsciously allowed to enter your intellectual, or conscious, mind.

If the results you presently have in your life are not exactly what you would like them to be, you can now see why. At the beginning of this cycle, you must have either chosen negative thoughts or allowed them to enter your mind. These thoughts then created images in your subconscious which over time took root and grew into your habits, beliefs, and conditioning. These negative habits, beliefs, and conditioning created negative emotions and feelings which led you to take the actions that created the results you do not totally like.

(Keep in mind that when I say "negative" thoughts or habits, I mean negative in the sense that they are not leading to the absolutely positive results you ideally would like in your life.)

The Y Factor - Part III

How to change any result in your life

The most exciting thing about the understanding you now have is that you now why and how you can change the results you are getting in your life to any results you would like to get.

If your thoughts create images which lead to feelings that cause actions that lead to results, you can change the results by changing the input on the front end of the process. This is what people mean when they say, "Change your mind, change your life." Here's how to do it:

> 1. Consciously choose a different, more effective, set of thoughts. Focus on thoughts of what you WANT, not what you don't want.
>
> 2. These thoughts will create a new set of images in your subconscious mind. As these images strengthen, your subconscious will go to work to create this new image in physical reality.
>
> 3. You'll experience a different set of feelings.
>
> 4. Your new feelings will lead you to a different set of actions that is in line with the new image you have created in your mind.
>
> 5. And, of course, these new actions will lead to a new, more positive set of results in your life.

Before we move on, one final reminder about expecting instant results.

Don't.

If you were building a house, you wouldn't expect the house to be done the day after you handed the blueprints to your architect. If you started on a workout program, you wouldn't expect to be in tip-top shape in two days (or at least you *shouldn't* expect that).

The Y Factor

WHY *you are where you are and how* **Y***ou can quickly and easily change any result in your life*

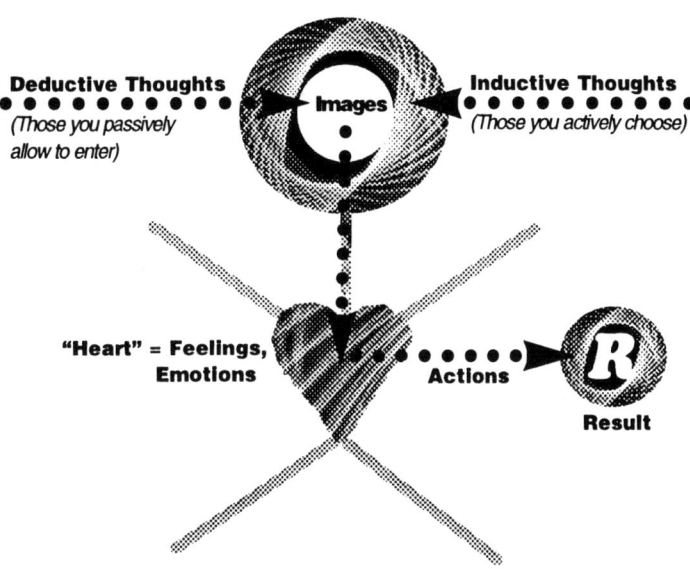

Deductive Thoughts
● ● ● ● ● ● ● ● ● ●
(Those you passively allow to enter)

Inductive Thoughts
● ● ● ● ● ● ● ● ● ●
(Those you actively choose)

Images

"Heart" = Feelings, Emotions

Actions

Result

How you get ALL results in your life:

1. Your mind thinks in pictures and your **THOUGHTS** control the **IMAGES** that form in your mind.
2. The new images determine the **FEELINGS** and **EMOTIONS** you experience.
3. You then naturally take new **ACTIONS** in harmony with your new image and new feelings.
4. Your actions create the **RESULTS** in your life.

To change ANY result in your life, follow 5 simple steps:

1. Change the original input by choosing a different set of **THOUGHTS**.
2. This forms new **IMAGES** in your mind.
3. The new images lead to new **FEELINGS** and **EMOTIONS.**
4. You then naturally take new **ACTIONS** in harmony with your new image and new feelings.
5. These new actions lead to new **RESULTS** in your life.

Stress-Free Success • 23

The same holds true for creating new results in your life. It is impossible to know exactly how strong the negative conditioning is in your subconscious mind. You have no idea how many thoughts and images contributed to strengthening it, so you don't know how much time or effort it will take to break it down.

What you do know, however, is just like with working out or building a house, if you keep moving forward, you WILL eventually get to your goal.

Lesson 4:
Decide Where You Want To Be

Quit dreamin' in color and livin' in black and white

Now that we have a good understanding of how we work and why we are where we are, we're ready to move on and start making the adjustments necessary to create our ideal life. The first step in this process is to decide exactly what that ideal life consists of FOR YOU. As that interminable baseball philosopher Yogi Berra once said, **"You've got to be very careful if you don't know where you're going because you might not get there."**

Knowing exactly where YOU want to go is an important point. Many people waste their entire lives pursuing someone else's dreams and go to the grave "with the music still in them" because they've never pursued their own. Make a promise to yourself that "**From this moment on, I joyfully choose MY OWN dreams, pursue MY OWN goals, and fulfill MY OWN potential.**" Each one of us has different talents and interests and all of our dreams will be somewhat different, although they may be very similar.

As we start this exciting process, keep the **Principle of the Blank Page** in mind:

> *The Principle of the Blank Page states that from this moment forward, your life is a blank page. NOTHING that has happened to you in the past has to affect you today, unless you want it to. You are the writer for your own script. You can create any kind of plot for your present and future that you choose. It's totally up to you. Best of all, you don't have to worry about a producer or anyone else editing your script. Whatever script you write is guaranteed, by*

Stress-Free Success • 25

universal natural law, to be acted out EXACTLY as you write it.

Focus on what you want, not what you have

As you begin the process of deciding what your ideal life should be like, don't fall into the common trap of basing your expectations on what you have in your life now or what you don't want to have in your life, either now or in the future. Instead, focus on ONLY what you DO want to have in your ideal life.

Don't underestimate the importance of these kinds of exercise. What you are doing is beginning to re-program your brain to think in terms of what you want in your life instead of what you don't want or what you already have.

Take a minute and think about how much time you spend focusing on what you don't want or don't like- the bad parts of your job or your boss, the problems with your kids or spouse, the aches and pains you feel.

Realize that every time you think about these things you are placing that image back into your subconscious mind. *Since your subconscious accepts exactly what you give it and goes to work immediately to turn these images into reality, what you are doing is creating a vicious circle in your life that virtually guarantees that you will only get more of the same results you are trying to avoid.*

What we are doing by thinking about the things we would like to have and experience in our ideal life is breaking the vicious prison that most of us get caught up in at some time in our lives.

What we do is think about the results we are getting in our lives today. These thoughts help form stronger images in our subconscious. This solidifies the habits, conditioning, and beliefs that led to our present results. We then have feelings based on these same habits, conditioning, and beliefs. If we are having the same feelings and emotions we've always had, we're probably going to continue doing the same things we've always done, which of course will lead us right back to the same results we've always received.

In effect, by focusing on our present results and letting these results dominate our thinking, we have almost guaranteed that the only thing we will get is more of the same results we already have. Refocusing our minds on what we WANT in our lives instead of what we already have breaks this loop.

We are consciously choosing different input at the top of the whole cycle. If our mind is focused on the ideal life we are creating, we can deposit images of this life into our subconscious. This creates a reservoir of mental experiences in our subconscious. Our subconscious will then go to work to do the only thing it can do- turn those images into reality. Over time, as we solidify the new images in our subconscious and break down the old ones, we will begin to experience new feelings and emotions. This will lead to new actions that will bring us the new results we are looking for.

This is why goal-setting and visualization are so important and why virtually every single winner in life engages in them on a daily basis.

As Albert Einstein once said,
"Imagination is more important than knowledge."

Every time we set a goal or visualize our ideal life, we are consciously choosing to focus on a positive thought. We can then take the next step and deposit this into our subconscious so that we are developing new images that lead to new beliefs, habits, and conditioning. These new beliefs, habits, and conditioning will NATURALLY cause us to feel a new set of emotions and take a new set of actions that leads to a new, much better set of results.

Notice that I emphasized the word "naturally." This is one of the most exciting benefits of this process. As you continue to form the images in your mind of you living your ideal lifestyle, you will begin to become more and more comfortable with you in that lifestyle and will begin to develop a stronger belief that you can in fact live this lifestyle. What you are doing is creating a new self-image that will naturally and spontaneously cause you to take new actions that will give you the new results you want in your life.

The critical role of Psycho-Cybernetics

As Dr. Maxwell Maltz so well described in his classic best-seller, *Psycho-Cybernetics*, our actions are a result of our self-image. Our self-image is a product of our habits, beliefs, and conditioning.

In his research, **Maltz found that we will naturally take actions that match our self-image.**

For example, if you thought of yourself as a shy, quiet person, you would probably be very fearful of meeting strangers and you would more than likely not enjoy cold calls to make sales.

If you thought of yourself as an outgoing, adventurous, confident person, you'd probably love meeting new people and would probably view cold calls as a welcome challenge and a chance to experience a new adventure in your life. In the first case, it would be natural for you to avoid cold calls at all costs.

In the second case, it would be perfectly natural for you to pick up the phone and make your calls without thinking twice about it. The only thing that changed was your self-image and this new self-image made an entirely different set of actions seem right and natural to you.

> *The key point to remember here is that **we naturally take actions that match our self-image.** Therefore, if we change our self-image, our actions will easily and naturally change right along with it. And we already*

know that if we start taking new actions, we ARE going to achieve new results.

This is the same process you are going through to create your ideal life. **Once your self-image totally matches the qualities of a person living your ideal life, you will find yourself spontaneously and naturally taking actions that support that self-image. And these actions will lead you quickly toward turning your ideal into a reality.**

For example, if one of the things on your list is to "earn $1,000,000 a year," and you now see yourself as a "$30,000 a year employee of Big Corporation," you need to make some adjustments. **Begin seeing yourself as you want to be, not as you are.** Build the image of you as a $1,000,000 a year producer. See the benefits of earning $1,000,000- where you can live, what you can buy, where you can travel, who you can help, what you can enjoy. As this image of you as a $1,000,000 per year producer becomes stronger, you will find yourself naturally taking actions that support your new self-image.

Immediately Create Your Million Dollar Image

Here's an easy way to speed this process along for anything you would like to experience in your life: **Ask yourself what a person in that position would feel or how they would act and then feel and act that way.** In this example, you would ask yourself "How would a person earning $1,000,000 feel and act?" A person with that kind of income would probably have all kinds of energy and be exuberant about enjoying life. He would have a smile on his face most of the time and not let little things bother him. He would be generous about sharing his wealth because he knows that he will always have plenty. He will invest time in causes that he believes in and in developing himself as a person.

If you're having trouble getting a clear image about how someone living your ideal life would feel and act, **look for a role model** that is living a life close to what you consider perfect. **Then model that person.** Be careful, though, that you model the good parts of this person and not the bad ones.

Now you have a good understanding of why it is important to focus on what you want to create in your life and not always stay focused on what you have already created, as so many of us do. Focusing on what you already have will create the vicious circle that guarantees that you will get more of the same. Focusing on what you want breaks this loop and sets your subconscious mind, your connecting link to the powers of Infinite Intelligence, to work to create these new results in your life.

Reach for YOUR B.U.D.
Never be afraid to reach for YOUR BUD - your "B"ig "U"ltimate "D"ream.

As John-Roger and Peter McWilliams, authors of the best-seller, *Do It*, said, **"If you're not playing a big enough game, you'll screw up the game you're playing just to give yourself something to do."**

> *John-Roger and Peter go on to say,* ***"The good news is that with every dream comes the time and the ability to fulfill it. The bad news? Many people use that time and ability doing something else- something that often has little or nothing to do with their dream."***

Don't be one of those people. **After all, you're going to spend the rest of your life doing something. It might as well be something that gets you excited and means something to you.** Choose your dreams and get started on them today. You'll be amazed at how the pieces of your dream puzzle begin to fall together when you make a decision to pursue YOUR dream. And I'd almost guarantee that your energy level will increase dramatically when you are using your energy to **pursue your own dream, not someone else's.**

Take the lid off
Now it's time to get crystal clear about what your dream really is and about what kind of life you really want to live so that you can start turning those dreams into reality. Get out a sheet of paper and invest 15 minutes answering these questions:

<u>For all the questions, assume that you are describing your IDEAL state, which has NOTHING to do with your present state.</u> Let yourself go and have some fun with this.

If time and money were no object, what would you do more of? Less of?

If you could be the best in the world at any one profession, what would it be? WHY?

If I gave you $10,000,000 cash right now, what three things would you do with it and how much would those things cost?

In 1 minute, describe the house you would build if you had $10,000,000 cash to build it.

What is your perfect vacation? How long? With whom? To where? What would you do there?

In 1 minute, describe the ideal love or family relationship for you. What would your partner and/or family be like? How much time would you spend with them? What would you most enjoy doing together? What kinds of values and beliefs would all of you have? What kinds of personalities?

If you could live anywhere in the world and bring your friends and family with you, where would it be?

If you could learn one new skill and knew you would become an expert at it, what would it be?

If you had $10,000,000 cash to anything you'd like, what would it be?

If you could change 1 thing about your life, what would it be?

If you could change 1 thing about yourself, what would it be?

In 3 minutes, describe the person you would become, if you could become anyone you want?
   What will you look like.... Think like.... Dress like.... I would do this work, have these values, have this personality

If one of your friends was describing you to a stranger who had never met you, what would you want them to say about you?

If two of your best friends were talking to each other about you, what would you want them to say?

Project 20 years into the future. If the Indianapolis Star were writing a front-page story about your life, what would you want the story to say about you?

How would you have spent your last 20 years?

What kind of person would it say you were?

If you knew you could not fail, what would you be doing each day? What hobbies would you pursue? What kind of career or business would you have? What kind of relationships would you build?

Where would you like to live? What city? What climate? Around what type of people or close to which specific people (this can be anybody, including celebrities)? Who would you like to live with? What would your relationship with these people be like?

How much do you really WANT to earn each year? What would be the ideal way to earn this money? How many hours would you work? What would you do?

EXACTLY what would you spend this money on? What would your house look like? How many rooms? How would it be decorated? What would the landscaping be like? Where would it be located?

If you could have any car ever built, what kind of car would you drive? How many cars would you have? Would you have a chauffeur and limo to drive you around?

Now that you've started the process of thinking in terms of what you WANT instead of what you have or what you think you can get, **make a master list of all the WANTS in your ideal life.**

Have some fun with this. **Get out your pencil right now and invest 15 minutes in brainstorming all the things YOU would like to experience in your perfect life.** Aim to have at least 50 things on your list at the end of the 15 minutes. This is not the time for censoring yourself so it if pops into your mind, write it down, no matter how crazy or unlikely you think it is.

Here are a few examples from my list that may help you get started:

> *Wake up to the crisp mountain air coming in the windows of my Tahoe retreat*
> *Invite my friends over to my own private island*
> *Build my dream home and office complex on a lake overlooking the mountains*
> *Build my own "Field of Dreams" baseball stadium in my yard*
> *Bench press 400 pounds*
> *Enjoy a professional massage whenever I would like*
> *Have my own art exhibit at an art gallery*
> *Ride bike along Great Wall in China*
> *Shoot native blow darts in Borneo*
> *Dance with partner to Fiddler on the Roof*
> *Help a child start his own business successfully*

> *Help a homeless person start their own business and buy a house*
> *Pitch in the World Series and pitch to Johnny Bench*
> *Shoot hoop with Michael Jordan*
> *Teach a direct marketing, writing, or publishing course at Northwestern*
> *Write a New York Times #1 best-seller*
> *Go on an African safari*
> *Ride a gondola through Venice*
> *Race camels between the pyramids of Egypt with my best friends*
> *Have a cover article written about me in Success magazine*
> *Study with the world's top martial arts master's*
> *Successfully build a foundation to teach the principles in this book to students, homeless, uneducated, single moms, and other groups who could really benefit from them*

The next two components of your ideal life

If you've answered those questions faithfully, you now have a pretty good picture of what your physical world will be like in your ideal life. Now let's move on to your emotional and spiritual worlds.

What kind of person will you have become in this ideal life? How will people describe you? Imagine that your local newspaper is writing a story about you. What would you like it to say about the kind of person you are and the things you have accomplished?

Here is an important question to answer: **If you could have one wish and you knew it would come true, what would it be?** (The one caveat is you can't wish for more wishes.)

> *If you're having trouble deciding on your answer to that question, close your eyes for a minute and imagine yourself at the Academy Awards. You are walking across stage to the thunderous standing ovation of the entire audience. People are beating on chairs,*

chanting, and clapping to show their support and appreciation for the role you have played. **What is that role?**

Did you end world hunger? Start a foundation to teach kids how to read? Raise the happiest, most loving family in the world? Find a way to teach everyone to live in a state of inner peace and realize the goodness and potential that is inside them? Serve as an example of personal excellence that others follow? Lead your church successfully in to a new millennium? Or thrill millions of viewers around the world with your ninth-inning home run to win the World Series?

Your answer to this question will tell you a lot about what direction you should be going in your life. Think about what percentage of your life today is taken up with activities that directly contribute to playing the role that you won your Academy Award for. If my guess is right, it's probably a very small percentage.

Don't criticize yourself, though. Remember the Principle of the Blank Page- from this moment forward, your life is a blank page and you can do anything with it you want. You can begin writing the script now that will allow you to play the role you will win your Academy Award for. In the rest of this book, you will learn how.

If you've never gone through an exercise like this, you may find it tough to answer some of these questions. That is very common, so don't worry about it. Most of us have been receiving messages that we can't have this or we can't do that for most of our lives. These messages have become firmly entrenched in our subconscious, and it will take some effort to overcome them. Don't get discouraged, however. Stick with this because it is vitally important.

After all, this is your life that you're designing and what would be more important than that?

Remember T-I, FAR?

> *Your Thoughts affect the Images in your subconscious which affect your Feelings that lead to your Actions that give you your results. Investing some time in exercises like these is breaking up the old Images that are not leading to the feelings, actions and results that you want.*

By thinking about exactly what your ideal life will be, you are consciously choosing positive thoughts that you can then use to create positive images that will lead to positive feelings and actions, and finally to the positive results that you dream of.

Build your dream book

Once you have your lists of what your ideal life will be like, you need a place to keep them so that you can refer to them regularly and begin building the images in your mind that will lead to their realization in your life.

One very effective way of doing this is to create a **Dream Book.** I have done this for years and it's been a lot of fun, as well as a wonderful tool to guide me down the road to my ideal life. **A Dream Book is a book that you create about everything that you want in your life.**

The way that I did it was to get a three-ring binder and a box of clear, plastic pages. Whenever I see pictures of the things I want in my life, I cut them out and put them in the plastic pages in the book. I have pictures of places to visit, the house I will build, painting and sculptures I like, people I will meet, causes I will contribute time or money to, books to read, and things I would like to experience.

Another helpful thing to include in your Dream Book is **your ideal daily schedule and ideal lifestyle**. Once you have this in mind, you can begin to do more of the things that contribute to your ideal schedule and lifestyle and less of those that don't contribute to it.

*A good way to do this is to **divide your week into 21 blocks. Morning, afternoon, and evening for each day. Then fill in what you would ideally like to be doing during those time blocks.*** Jot down when you would like to get up and go to bed each day. Who you would like to spend time with. What projects you would like to work on. When you would like to exercise or get your massage.

Here is one possible table of contents for your own Dream Book or Book of Ideal Life:

- *Places I will travel*
- *Things I will experience*
- *People I will meet*
- *Things I will own (house, cars, boats, planes, clothes, your own island, etc)*
- *Accomplishments I will do*
- *My ideal day, week, month, and year*
- *My ideal mental, emotional, spiritual, and physical state*
- *What I will contribute to the world*
- *What causes or ideas I will help out and how I will help them*
- *List of books to read and knowledge I will acquire*
- *My long list of goals*
- *My Big Ultimate Dream (BUD)*
- *My Primary Overall Goal (POG)*
- *My Life's Focus or Mission Statement*
- *My Personal Creed*

(These last four you will learn about in the next few chapters.)

Remember, this is YOUR Book of YOUR Ideal Life. It should contain those images and statements that are meaningful to YOU. If you don't really get into travel, don't include places to travel in your book. If your church is one of the major focuses in your life, create an entire section of goals and dreams related to your church.

The bottom line is, customize your book so that you get excited and emotionally involved with it every time you open it. That's the key to making your Book an effective part of your plan for creating your ideal life.

Now that you have your Book started, let's move on to the foundation for your ideal life: your life's focus or mission statement and your personal creed for living a successful life.

Lesson 5:
Develop A Solid Foundation For Achieving Your Goals With Your Life's Focus Statement & Personal Creed

Your Life's Focus

Now that you have a good idea of what your ideal life will look like, it's time to determine what broad direction you want your life to move in and what kind of person you must become in order to live this life. One good way to do this is to write **your life's focus statement, also called your statement of purpose, or mission statement.**

You've probably heard all kinds of "talk" about mission statements and their importance, but if you're like most of us, you really don't have a good idea about what a focus or mission statement is, why you need a mission statement, or how you go about developing one.

Why do you need a Life's Focus Statement?

Your focus or mission statement is your guide to help you stay on track to fulfilling your potential and living your dreams. It gives you a simple test to decide what actions to take to lead you along the proper path for your life. It also serves as a yardstick to measure yourself with.

Having a clearly defined mission simplifies your decision-making process by serving as a guiding principle that helps you choose among alternative courses of action.

For example, part of my mission statement is "to be an example of maximum personal excellence." Now at times, I just feel like saying "screw it all" and curling up on the couch for a nice afternoon nap. When I'm in this mood, I just ask myself, "Would a person with the mission of becoming 'an example of maximum personal excellence' pitter the afternoon away on the couch or would he push himself a little bit and finish his writing for the day?" Obviously, he would finish his writing, so that's exactly what I do. The funny thing is, when I frame my decisions in this way, it seems perfectly natural to finish my writing instead of taking a nap because finishing my writing is an action in harmony with my mission. Taking a nap is not.

Focus or mission statements can also help you decide what to pursue and what to give up in your life. For example, the second part of my mission is to "create opportunities for others to enjoy maximum personal excellence, growth, happiness, fulfillment, and understanding." Obviously, there are many ways to accomplish this part of my mission.

For example, I used to own and run a successful marketing consulting business. I realized, though, that there were parts of my marketing consulting business that I did not feel were the best way to accomplish this part of my mission. Yes, they did help others build their businesses and so indirectly, they were "creating opportunities for other to enjoy growth, happiness, and fulfillment," but I believed that there was another way that would allow me to fulfill my mission even better.

This allowed me to give up most of my marketing clients and not worry about the temporary dip in my personal income or the emotions of shifting career focus. I knew that by investing more of my time and resources in writing, publishing, and teaching, I would be fulfilling my mission in a higher and better way.

What I found when I made this decision was that it released all kinds of energy that had been bottled up in doing things solely because I was naturally good at them and they made money instead of doing them because I was good at them and they contributed to living my values and my mission. And, in the long run, I'll make more from publishing one best-selling book than from years of marketing consulting anyway.

What about destiny?

At this point, many people ask me, "You're sitting there telling me I have all this control over everything in my life but sometimes I have trouble believing it. Sometimes it seems as if things just happen - as if there is some kind of pre-destiny that is determining what happens in my life independently of my thoughts or decisions. Is there a such thing as destiny and how does it affect what I am learning?"

That's a very good question.

The answer is, you do have a destiny, if you so choose. You are a physical expression of creative spirit. As such, there are some broad brush strokes that indicate the general direction your life will probably take. How you respond to these broad strokes is up to you.

Imagine that you are a painter and are about ready to create a mural titled, "My Perfect Life." You settle down in front of your canvas and get all your paints arranged. You have some excellent ideas in your head and you're excited to get started. You look up at the canvas and your mouth drops. You forgot that you had already put a series of broad brush strokes across the canvas when you were playing around a few days earlier. You aren't quite sure what to do. You know that there isn't a single other blank canvas that large in the entire city, and you're anxious to get started on "My Perfect Life." You now have a decision to make.

You can either accept the broad brush strokes that are already there and work them into your painting, thereby creating a complete work of beauty from the few broad strokes that you had to start with. Or, you can say, "Yuck, I've changed my mind. Those colors and patterns are sick and I don't like them." In that case, you would paint over the broad brush strokes and change them. It's your painting and the decision is up to you. Work with the broad strokes that are already there or paint over the and create an entirely new picture from scratch.

That is the role destiny plays in your life. What we sometimes call destiny can be thought of as a broad brush stroke. It may say that you have a tendency to be better at athletics or you have a natural gift for writing or you have a brilliant mind for numbers. Those are the broad brush strokes. It's up to you if you incorporate them into "My Ideal Life" or leave them out and use a whole different set of patterns.

You make the decision about whether or how to use your broad brush strokes. Just because you can outrun everyone in your class doesn't mean you have to become an Olympic sprinter. You are perfectly free to invest your time into becoming a world-class writer instead, of that's what interest you and gets you "juiced" about life.

Focus vs. Mission

That is why at the beginning of this section, I called this project your Life's Focus or mission statement.

> *Many people think of a mission statement as a permanent, God-given thing that they must rigidly follow forever. Often, it easier to think in terms of your life's focus. You choose what you would like to focus your life on today, based on your current level of awareness. If you later reach a higher level that makes you aware of a new direction you would like your life to move in, you are free to change your Life's Focus to reflect your new awareness.*

This entire process that you are going through as you work through the exercises in this book will help you make that decision. Just stay relaxed and allow the decision to be revealed to you. This is a creative process and creative processes cannot be forced. They must be allowed to happen.

And, remember, you are the one doing the painting. "My Ideal Life" is your creation. There is no right and wrong way to paint your masterpiece. If you don't like part of it, just go back and change the brush strokes. Paint over the part you don't like and replace it with something you feel better about.

Let yourself go and let it flow. The result will be a masterpiece of life that you and all those around you will admire for years to come.

How do you create your Life's Focus Statement?

Now that you have a good idea of what a focus or mission statement is and what role it plays in your life, the next question is how you go about creating your own mission statement. Start with answering this one simple question:

"What am I willing to dedicate my life to?"

Think about that for a moment. What are you really willing to dedicate your life to? Eliminating world hunger? Finding a cure for cancer? Helping others enjoy more inner peace? Making others laugh and smile? Helping people achieve financial independence?

I recently read a story about Mother Teresa. The reporter had asked her why she did what she did. She said simply that her mission was to help others die more peacefully. And she dedicated her entire life to doing just that.

As you continue to learn about this idea, you'll see that many people's Life's Focus contain an element of helping others. This is because your nature is like Nature. It abhors a vacuum. Whenever something is given away, it is replaced with something else. When a river "gives away" its water to the ocean, more water rushes in to fill the space. When you open the windows of your car to let the hot air out, cool air rushes in to replace it. Giving to others works the same way. **When you give, you temporarily create a "hole" which cannot stay empty. It is immediately filled with something. If you give goodness and caring, your "hole" is filled with goodness and caring.**

I would suggest keeping this simple rule in mind when choosing your focus or mission. You don't have to dedicate your entire life to giving to or helping others. In fact, that would create an imbalance with other consequences we'll discuss later. It is healthy and right to dedicate a portion of your life to giving to and helping others, however.

As I mentioned, my mission is "to make my life an example of maximum personal excellence and to create opportunities for others to enjoy the same." This gives a balance between my personal growth and helping others.

Get out a sheet of paper and begin sketching out ideas for your life's mission. Don't expect to hit on your perfect mission immediately. Just jot down ideas and play with them until you have something that "feels right" to YOU. It took me almost two years of working with my mission before I had it phrased exactly the way I wanted it.

Here's how to create your own Statement:

1. Answer the question, "What am I willing to dedicate my life to?"

2. Imagine yourself at the Academy Awards. What role are they giving you an award for playing in your life?

3. When you answered the question earlier about what one wish you would choose if I could grant you any wish you wanted, what did your answer tell you about what you feel is really important? What kind of mission might support this feeling?

Take 10 minutes and brainstorm answers to these three questions. When you're done, you should have a good feeling for the right general area for your mission or life's purpose. To help you with phrasing your mission in a way that is meaningful to you, here are some starters:

My mission is to teach others to...

My mission is to learn and to grow...

The focus of my life is to provide... for ....

The focus of my life is to make a difference by...

My purpose is to have fun and live life as an adventure...

My purpose is to create joy for myself and others...

My mission is to help others understand themselves better through creative expression of myself...

When you have a focus or mission statement that feels "right" to you, write out two clean copies of it. Put one on your desk top, your refrigerator, your bathroom mirror, or some other place that you will see it regularly. Take the second copy and add it to your Perfect Life Book.

Review your focus or mission statement at least once a day until it is ingrained in your mind. Keep revising it until the phrasing is the way that you want it. Make a commitment to live your mission daily.

When you are making decisions, ask yourself, "What would a person with my mission do in this situation?" Then do it, joyously, and without hesitancy because you know it is the right decision for you.

Develop a Personal Creed

You've now decided on your life's focus and know what ultimate direction you would like your life to move in. What you're probably thinking now is, "That's all fine and dandy, but seems kind of abstract. How can I put these ideas in concrete terms that I can use every day?" That is the function of your Personal Creed.

Your Personal Creed is a concise set of guidelines for you to follow that will make it easy to make decisions and take actions that are in harmony with your beliefs and values and which help you live your mission or life's purpose.

Basically, your Personal Creed is the rules you set up to play your Game of Life. Following them means you win the game and not following them means you don't win. Nice and simple. Without a Personal Creed, you could be winning and feel like you're losing because the rules are unfair.

So, how do you go about out creating your Personal Creed? Start by writing down the answer to these questions:

"What are your rules for being happy?"

"What will you do and what won't you do in your life?"

"What are your guidelines for a successful life":

"How will you know if you're living your mission and your values?"

What you are doing is coming up with some simple rules that you can use to make decisions and lead your life. These are **YOUR rules.** There are no right and wrong. The important thing is that you decide what will make you happy and will give you an inner sense of integrity and peace. Then make those things a part of your creed and COMMIT to living that creed EVERY DAY.

To help you, here is a sample of how you may write your personal creed:

Your Personal Creed for a Successful Life

Go first class
Don't mountain climb over mole hills
Do what others are not willing to do
Do the tough things first and the rest will be easy
It's never too late to start
Always go the extra mile
Keep commitments
To get somewhere you have to leave somewhere
Progress involves risk. You can't steal second with your foot on first
Hurry up and be patient. Hustle while you wait
Don't become too busy driving to take time to get gas
Sharpen the saw regularly

Tell them "We're so glad you're in the game."
Don't love their actions. Love the person.
Don't just feed them; teach them to fish.
Let me listen to you first.
LIVE until I die.
Play my own game and keep my own score.
Keep life simple.
Enjoy the process.
Make work play but don't play at work.
Keep a smile on my face and in my heart.
Demand more of myself than anyone demands of me.
Become in order to attract and deserve.
Invest all of my past in today.
Take responsibility.
Excuses don't count.
No limits.
Put up the walls on my foundations.
Let go of the old to make room for the new.
Do that at which you're the best and delegate the rest.
Cross the middle line.
Remember the people involved.
Never judge.
Choose how I think, how I feel, and how I react.
Give and receive love abundantly.
Act from desire for gain, not fear of loss
Stay balanced.
Sow before I reap.
Always be the student and the teacher.
Strengthen mind and body daily.
See rainbows in thunderstorms.
Relax and let the higher powers guide me.
ALWAYS play by MY rules.

To give you some more ideas about how to develop your personal creed for living a successful life, let me give you two more examples of creeds developed by well-known leaders.

Your creed can be very simple.

When **John Wooden**, coach of the great UCLA basketball teams and one of the winningest coaches in basketball history, completed grade school, his father gave him a seven-point creed, which he says he still lives by every day of the year.

> **John Wooden's 7-Point Creed**
> 1. Be true to yourself.
> 2. Make each day your masterpiece.
> 3. Help others.
> 4. Drink deeply from good books.
> 5. Make friendship a fine art.
> 6. Build a shelter against a rainy day.
> 7. Pray for guidance and give thanks every day.

Napoleon Hill, author of the all-time classic, *Think and Grow Rich*, shared his personal creed in his follow-up bestseller, *The Master Key to Riches*.

> **A Happy Man's Creed**
> *I have found happiness by helping others to find it.*
> *I have sound physical health because I live temperately in all things, and eat only the foods which Nature requires for body maintenance.*
> *I am free from fear in all of its forms.*
> *I hate no man, envy no man, but love all mankind.*
> *I am engaged in a labor of love with which I mix play generously. Therefore I never grow tired.*
> *I give thanks daily, not for more riches, but for wisdom with which to recognize, embrace and properly use the great abundance of riches I now have at my command.*
> *I speak no name save only to honor it.*
> *I ask no favors of anyone except the privilege of sharing my riches with all who will receive them.*

> *I am on good terms with my conscience. Therefore it guides me correctly in all that I do.*
>
> *I have no enemies because I injure no man for any cause, but I benefit all with whom I come into contact by teaching them the way to enduring riches.*
>
> *I have more material wealth than I need because I am free from greed and covet only that material things I can use while I live.*
>
> *I own a great estate which is not taxable because it exists mainly in my own mind in intangible riches which cannot be assessed or appropriated except by those who adopt my way of life. I created this vast estate by observing Nature's laws and adapting my habits to conform therewith.*

Notice a couple things about Hill's and Wooden's creeds: first, they are very personal and reflect their own unique view of life. They contain statements that are meaningful to them and it doesn't matter what others think of them.

Second, following their creeds will help them live a BALANCED life. The creeds contain elements of health, personal development, wealth, and spirituality. Following all the points in the creed will automatically mean that they will live a prosperous life with an abundance of health, relationship, spiritual, and material riches.

Now go back to your draft of your personal creed and invest one hour in really thinking about how you want to live your life - what rules you want to set for living a successful life. Revise and re-work your creed until each point in it feels "right" to you.

When you are done, read through the entire creed and ask yourself, **"If I followed all of the points in my creed would I be living a life that is congruent with my mission? Would I be following my own values and beliefs and not those that others try to tell me to follow or adopt? Would following this creed**

naturally lead to what I would call a successful life?"

If you answered yes to these questions, you are now light years ahead of the average American. Hold on to your seat because **you are ready to make a quantum leap forward toward turning ALL your dreams into reality.**

You've accomplished a lot so far, so take a break now and reward yourself with something nice you have been wanting for a while - a nice dinner at a posh restaurant, a professional massage, a new CD, or whatever will symbolize accomplishment to you.

Now that you're back, let me share a couple more thoughts with you before we move on.

The first is about breaking out of your comfort zone. Just taking the initiative to write down your dreams, your mission, and your personal creed probably took you way out of your comfort zone.

Now that you've finished those steps doesn't it feel good to look back on what you accomplished and know that you're moving forward rapidly? That's the feeling you will get each time you break out of your comfort zone. Start to view testing your comfort zone as fun.

Realize that the only way to grow is to get temporarily uncomfortable. If you're not a least a little uncomfortable, you're not growing. Resolve to get uncomfortable regularly and to enjoy being uncomfortable. Here's something to help:

Breaking out of your comfort zone
"I used to have a comfort zone where I knew I couldn't fail.
The same four walls and busy work were really more like jail.
I longed so much to do the things I'd never done before,
But I stayed inside my comfort one and paced the same old floor.

I said it didn't matter that I wasn't doing much.
I said I didn't care for things like diamonds, cars and such,

*I claimed to be so busy with the things inside the zone,
But deep inside I kept longing for some victory of my own*

*I couldn't let my life go by just watching others win!
I held my breath and stepped outside to let the change begin.
I took a step and with new strength I'd never felt before,
I kissed my comfort zone good bye and closed and locked the door.*

*If you are in a comfort zone afraid to venture out,
Remember that all winners at one time were filled with similar doubt.
A step or two and words of praise can make your dreams come true.
Greet your future with a smile -- success is there for you."*

Do one thing today that stretches your comfort zone. Then one more tomorrow. And each day thereafter. At the end of one month, you'll have stretched your comfort zone in 30 new ways and I'd be willing to bet that you have one heck of a lot bigger comfort zone than you used to.

A warning before we move on:
You are living your own life. No one else can live it for you. When you develop your mission statement, your personal creed, your goals, and your definitions of success and happiness, you are setting up the rules for the game of life that you are playing. You can set any rules you want. Set rules that YOU <u>WANT</u> to play by.

Lesson 6:
Adopt A Stress-Free Belief System That Makes It Easier To Achieve Your Goals

As we discussed earlier, your results are a product of the images in your subconscious mind which lead to emotions that trigger the actions that produce the results. The images are created by thousands of thoughts which enter your subconscious mind each minute.

It follows then, that if you can place the proper thoughts into your mind, your mind will take care of producing the proper images. These images will lead to the emotions and actions necessary to achieve your goals.

The way to make this whole process easy and natural is to adopt a set of guiding beliefs that productive and empowering instead of destructive and limiting. That is what you will learn in this section.

Incorporating empowering beliefs into your life

Each of us will hold slightly different beliefs based on our culture, our conditioning, and the other influences in our lives. Think for a minute about what beliefs you have in these areas:

- Spiritual or religious
- Sex and relationships, including family
- Money and finances
- Career
- Health and exercise

Get out a piece of paper and jot down what you believe in each of these areas. Be brutally honest with yourself. Since your beliefs are a primary component of your actions and your actions create the results in your life, **you can easily tell what your beliefs are by looking at the results you are getting.**

Invest a few minutes thinking about this idea. It will help you understand yourself much better. Think about what beliefs you must have to create the results you are getting in your life. Sometimes what you think you believe (or think you should believe) is not what you really believe when you think about it.

And, oftentimes, you do believe one thing, but another belief you hold overrides it and negates it. For example, if you are fat, you might not really believe that eating low-fat foods is important. Or you might believe a low-fat diet is good, but at the same time have a stronger belief that you deserve to "indulge" in cakes and cookies at every meal or that you don't have enough willpower to turn down junk food.

Now take out a clean piece of paper and write the five categories above across the top of a page. Under each one, write down what kinds of beliefs you must adopt in order to live your ideal life and fulfill your mission. Ask yourself questions like these:

- **What beliefs would a person who was living my ideal life hold?**
- **What beliefs would a person who was fulfilling my mission hold?**
- **What beliefs would allow me to enjoy the most happiness without conflicting with my values?**

The 4 keys to powerful beliefs

While you are doing this exercise, keep the following four keys to powerful beliefs in the back of your mind:

1. Act from desire for gain, not fear of loss.

First, <u>act from desire for gain, not fear of loss</u>. Go after what you want to have in your life, instead of hanging on to what you don't want to lose.

Give up everything in your life that relates to fear of loss. For example, go after your perfect relationship instead of hanging on to an average one just to avoid temporarily losing the feeling of being in a loving relationship. Go after your perfect business or career instead of hanging on to a job you don't like just to avoid temporarily losing income.

Focusing on what you want to gain, instead of what you don't want to lose has two key benefits for you. First, you will be keeping your mind on positive thoughts which will create positive images in your subconscious and translate into positive results in your life.

And, by releasing everything in your life that is "average", you will be making room in your life for the things that are "outstanding." You cannot develop an "outstanding" relationship unless you release your "average" one. You cannot develop a perfect career or business unless you release your average one. You cannot develop a better way of reacting to others and expressing your love for them unless you release your mediocre ones. This is true for everything in your life.

Nature abhors a vacuum. *When you release the average or mediocre things in your life, the space you create will be filled with something. Why not give it room to be filled with the absolute best life has to offer by releasing everything else from your life?*

If you are focused on the good that you want the space to be filled with, you will attract the resources you need to create an "outstanding" life that gets you totally juiced about getting out of bed in the morning instead of an "average" humdrum, boring, just-getting-by existence.

2. Adopt an abundance mentality

The second key to powerful beliefs that will help you create your ideal life is to adopt an **abundance mentality**. This means to look at the world and everything in it with the view that **there is plenty for everyone**.

This is a switch from the message that many of us have been programmed with. School attempts to teach us that only a few kids can get straight "A's" or star on the football team. Mass media tries to convince us that only a few people with "perfect bodies" will enjoy sexual attraction. Our parents often imbibe us with the idea that "money doesn't grow on trees," which really means there is a limited amount of it and we'd better hang on to what little we can get.

We also get many messages subconsciously telling us that because there is only a limited pie that we are eating from, by earning something for ourselves, we are depriving someone else. If we earn a bunch of money, we must have kept someone else from earning it. If we love ourselves too much, we won't have any love left for others.

Not.

The truth of the matter is, there is plenty to go around.

The pie we are living from is universal and infinite. When we enjoy our share of the pie, we never deprive anyone else of their share. Think of it in this way. Whenever you enjoy a bite of the pie of life, this is your reward for your contribution to making the pie bigger for everyone.

This is especially true for wealth and love. **All wealth really is is the expression of an idea that changes something into a form with a higher and better use.**

Oil is changed into fuel for our cars. Sand is changed into silicon chips to make computers. Electromagnetic force is changed into electricity that lights our homes. Iron ore is changed into steel that builds our cars. Clay is fired and turned into bricks that build our homes.

Think about this for a minute.

The men who created oil, computer, auto, and real estate empires became some of the wealthiest men on this planet. Did they take wealth away from anyone else? No.

What they did was expand the pie so that all of us could benefit. A much larger pie means that by creating the companies that paid them a fortune, they also created billions of dollars of additional wealth that we can all benefit from.

Another important point to remember- **everything we need to create great wealth for ourselves is already here. All we have to do is become aware of the idea for changing one thing into a higher and better form**. The developers of oil wells, real estate deals, auto empires, and huge computer companies didn't "produce" anything "new." All they really did was take something that already existed and change it from one form into a better form. And they (as well as thousands of others) made billions of dollars because of it.

Not a bad deal, huh?

Begin viewing wealth in this way. Brainstorm ideas you can use to expand the pie for everyone. **As you expand the pie for others, you will create great wealth for yourself as well.**

The same idea works for love, also. Love is our highest expression of our spiritual nature. If we are "created in the image and likeness of God," why would God limit our capacity to love?

> *Do you really think humans are built with some kind of love-meter that says, "Oh, oh, watch out, Fred, you're reaching your love limit. You better step back. Maybe you shouldn't love yourself as much because, gee, that'll just about use up all your capacity and you won't have any love left for your kids, Freida" ? I highly doubt it.*

Try this experiment. **Take the lid off your capacity to love.** Think of yourself as an expression of God or spirit who has an infinite capacity to love. Love yourself wholeheartedly and love those around you wholeheartedly and don't worry about how much love you're giving out because there's ALWAYS plenty more capacity inside of you.

To review the second key to powerful beliefs:

> ***Adopt an abundance mentality.***
> *Quit viewing the world as a zero-sum game with limits on the amount of wealth, love and other resources that are in it. Take the lid off your beliefs and give and receive love and wealth abundantly because there's more than enough to go around.*

3. Take responsibility for where you are- but don't let it affect where you're going

You are where you are. That's all. Period.

Try not to attach labels to things. Accept where you are at this present moment without labeling it as "not where you'd like to be" or "sad" or "terrible.". **The present moment just is. The only way it can be bad is if you decide it is bad. It is entirely up to you. You can also decide that it's good - or neutral - or whatever else you choose.**

In fact, you are perfectly free to choose exactly how you want to think about anything that is occurring in your life now or has occurred in the past. Exercise your freedom in a positive manner by choosing to view everything that happens in your life as part of a great adventure that is moving toward the most perfect possible path for you.

Life is not random. Things happen for a reason. If you view the reason that everything happens as good, you'll quickly be able to eliminate most of your so-called "pains" and "evils" from your life.

> *And, by all means,* ***lose this stupid attitude that the world is out to get you. The world is not out to get you.*** *In fact, most of the world has no idea you even exist, and the small part of the world that does*

Stress-Free Success • 58

know you exist is generally too caught up in their own affairs to care much about "getting you."

I would recommend adopting one of two viewpoints: you can either quit labeling evens altogether and just accept them for what they are, without judging them as good or bad.

Or, you can acknowledge that it is very difficult to live in a modern, complex society without making any judgments, and so choose to judge only in a positive way by viewing the world with the attitude that "everything happens for a good reason and in every temporary challenge is the seed of a much greater good, so I will always find the seed and use it to plant the greater good."

Not allowing the past to keep its grip on you also frees up energy for you to create the future you dream of. Every time you remember the "bad" things that have happened to you in the past, you are reinforcing the images in your subconscious mind. Your subconscious, being the obedient servant that it is, will then go to work to re-create these same types of "bad" experiences in your life because that is what you are focused on and expect to happen.

Viewing events as "processes leading to higher good for myself and others around me" allows you to break the negative patterns of the past. Every time you focus on a positive thought about something, you are breaking up your negative conditioning and replacing it with positive conditioning that will allow you to naturally and effortlessly take the actions that will lead to positive results in your life.

4. Do what YOU can do; don't worry about the rest

The final key to developing a powerful belief system is to choose beliefs and options that YOU can do something about personally.

It **IS** your responsibility to be the best person YOU can be and serve as an example to others. **It is not your**

responsibility to change the world, or even one other person in it. You know as well as I do that is entirely futile. All you can change is yourself, and that is right and good.

The Secret To Stress-Free Success

Choose direct alternatives in your life is the secret of the stress-free part of stress-free success. Direct alternatives are those in which you make the decision about how things will turn out. Indirect alternatives are when you try to change the attitude of others so they will do what you want.

For example, suppose you feel that your taxes are too high. An indirect alternative would be to waste hundreds of hours trying to start a campaign to lower them. A direct alternative would be to invest your time in earning more money so you still had plenty left after paying taxes or to find a way to legally avoid paying them in the first place.

Suppose you are a student who feels that the curriculum in your school is not up to par. An indirect alternative would be to waste hundreds of hours trying to convince the administration and your professors to change the curriculum. A direct alternative would be to change schools or go to the library and research the subjects you want to learn more about on your own.

Imagine you are a salesperson who wants to sell 10 widgets to provide a nice income for your family. An indirect alternative would be to waste time trying to convince everyone on the street that they need your widgets. A direct alternative would be to locate people whose self-interest would be satisfied by buying your widget and then show them clearly how their self-interest would be served by purchasing your widget.

This concept of indirect and direct alternatives has led to a bad rap for positive thinking in some circles. In many cases, people try to use their own positive thinking to create a reality that is dependent upon the specific decisions of other people. Don't fall into this trap.

You CAN use positive thinking to create positive images that lead to positive results in your life, but **don't waste your time trying to determine exactly HOW those results will come about. It is your responsibility to choose the outcome. It is the responsibility of your subconscious mind, in partnership with Spirit and Infinite Intelligence, to determine HOW the result will come about.**

Thinking in indirect alternatives makes you waste your life trying to remake others. Trust yourself.

> *When you are assessing a situation, ask yourself, "Is this a situation I can personally do something about and is this what I want for myself? Does it fit with my values and mission?" If you answered yes, then relax and enjoy it to the max. If you answered no, the relax and look elsewhere for a better situation.*

Now that you understand the importance of direct alternatives, we need to find out what's holding us back.

Most of our lives can be compared to a hot air balloon sitting on the ground straining against its ropes. As soon as the ropes are released, it rises smoothly and effortlessly into the bright blue sky. When more lift is needed, the pilot throws out sandbags and the change in weight in the balloon allows it to continue its effortless climb.

We're the same way. Our natural state is to soar high in the sky, just like the hot air balloon, but most of us are holding ourselves back by tying ropes to the balloon and not releasing our sandbags. Before we can throw out all the "sandbags" in our lives, we must first become aware of where the sandbags are.

Then, we'll develop a strategy to get rid of them so that our lives can soar smoothly into the heavens, just like the hot air balloon. We'll begin by examining our overall views of the world, commonly called our "paradigms."

Lesson 7:
Eliminate the stress-causing beliefs you now hold

The power of paradigms

Our paradigms (pronounced pair-uh-dimes) are our view of the world and our beliefs about how things around us work and how "they really are."

Since everything around us is constantly changing, our paradigm is really our current perception about "reality." It affects every bit of our lives because the way we view the world determines what thoughts will enter our conscious mind and therefore what images will form in our subconscious. You already know that your subconscious will immediately go to work to turn the images it is given into physical reality, so our paradigm is critical in determining what actions we will take on a daily basis, and therefore, what results we will receive in our lives.

Since our paradigm plays such an important role in the kind of life we live, one of the best ways to determine what "sandbags" we need to eliminate from our lives is to examine our paradigm, or frame of reference for life. By examining our overall view of the world, we can figure out what areas are working for us and what areas are actually holding us back.

As **Stephen Covey** said in *Principle-Centered Leadership*, "**If you want to make slow, incremental improvement, change your attitude or behavior. But if you want to improve in major ways - if you want to make quantum improvements, change your frame of reference [your paradigm].**"

Think for a minute what happens when you change your frame of reference, or paradigm:

> 1. First, you will obviously have an entirely new set of conscious thoughts.
> 2. Then, your subconscious will also filter information in your environment in an entirely new way.
> 3. Together, these changes will cause new images to be formed in your subconscious.
> 4. The new images will trigger a new set of emotions and feelings.
> 5. These new emotions and feelings will guide you toward a new set of actions. Since these actions will be congruent with your new paradigm, or frame of reference, they will seem natural to you and you will have no trouble taking them.
> 6. As you continue behaving in this new way, your actions will naturally lead to new results in your life.

This is the same process that Christopher Columbus went through when he discovered America. Before he sailed, it was "common sense" wisdom that the world was flat. Everyone "knew" that was true and people behaved accordingly. Old Chris decided, however, that this paradigm was flawed and he opted to adopt a new frame of reference.

His belief that the world was not flat led him to an entirely new set of questions. He asked, "How can I sail around the world?" instead of "How far can I go before I fall off the side of the earth?"

He formed an image in his mind of himself sailing successfully around the world and discovering new trade routes and trading partners. He became emotionally involved with this idea and would not give it up.

Despite the ridicule he received from his "educated" peers who "knew" he was wrong, Columbus persisted.

The image in his mind and the emotions it triggered made it natural for him to continue to take action to prepare for his voyage. Finally, he convinced the Queen to outfit his ships and as they say, the rest is history.

Columbus' successful voyage changed the paradigm and lives of people around the world so we now act under a frame of reference that "knows" that the world is round.

On an everyday basis, you can make dramatic changes in your own life by changing the paradigm you work under.

Before you can successfully do this, you need to understand the "common sense" paradigms that many of us have adopted that are actually not "common sense" at all.

In fact, when you look at the truth behind them, ***most of what we call "common sense" is just a bunch of misleading frames of references designed to turn us all into a bunch*** *of "common", everyday people. Now, if being just like the majority of those you see around you is okey-dokey with you, put this book down and go enjoy your meager life. If, however, you are ready to throw out your sandbags and allow your life to soar with the eagles, prepare to move on.*

Lies We've Been Sold
In this section, we'll examine the lies we've been sold.

The 7 biggest lies we've been told about the world around us...

Lie #1: "I can't do it"
Many of us are holding ourselves back by believing that others have innate talents and abilities that we do not possess and could never develop. This is not true. **We all come from the same source and have the same potential.** The way we develop that potential is up to us.

Stress-Free Success • 65

Yes, it is true that some of us are born with certain physical and mental tendencies that seem to give us an advantage in certain areas. That does not mean, however, that others cannot level the playing field by using the laws of Nature and of Mind to develop a set of talents that will function just as well as those of the "natural."

> One of the best examples of this is baseball great Pete Rose. He was not blessed with the natural talent of being able to hit a baseball well. But he decided that that's what he wanted to do. This put thoughts into his conscious mind. Every day he built images of himself rapping out base hit after base hit. He got emotionally involved with these ideas and it became second nature to take the actions necessary - to stay on the practice field hours after everyone else left, to take an extra hour of batting practice when his hands were already raw with blisters, to watch videotapes of his swing and learn from his coaches, to be focused on improving his game daily. The result? Pete Rose, a rather average guy with rather average baseball talent, retired with more hits than any other player in the 125-year history of baseball.

Next time you find yourself thinking, "Gee, I'd sure like to do that, but I can't," ask yourself...

"Why do I believe I can't?
Is there a rational reason for my belief?
Could I be mistaken in the belief?"
Then ask, "How CAN I accomplish this?"

Make a list of all the possible ways that you could accomplish your goal even if most of them seem totally outrageous or "impossible" at this time. What you will find with most situations is that by shifting your paradigm to "There is a way," you will find the way and "can't" will lose its power and turn into "can."

Lie #2: "Things need fixing"

Ninety-nine percent of the things you think need fixing are just fine the way they are. They need to be understood, not fixed. When you understand how they really work, you'll realize that most often, they're not broken. **What is messed up is your perception of the situation, not the situation itself.**

This is especially true in multi-person organizations. We have a whole legion of so-called consultants, management experts, and "leaders" who are going around trying to "fix" organizations. For the most part, it's not working.

Why?

They're acting under the paradigm that if an organization or a relationship within that organization is broken, they can find the problem, get the right part, stick it in, turn it on, and the whole thing will work all hunky-dorey. Not. What their paradigm fails to take into account is that any organization or relationship is made up of individual people, all of whom are functioning with different paradigms, sets of beliefs, and types of conditioning. It is impossible to "find" a problem and "fix" it in this type of complex structure. **Trying to solve people problems with this thing mentality is like sticking square blocks into round holes.**

A waste of time because it doesn't work. What needs to be done is to understand each of the people involved and then develop solutions that take into consideration the uniqueness of each individual.

Don't fall into this same trap in your relationships. The latest "fix" that you read in a magazine or see on the news may indeed work for some people, but **don't assume that it will work for you until you try it for yourself. On the other hand, don't assume it won't work for you until you try it for yourself.**

Approach everything like an experimental scientist. First, get a good understanding of the other person and their set of beliefs, values, and the way they look at the world. Then, work together to understand how both of you would like the relationship to work. Build this image of a perfect relationship in both of your minds and turn it over to your subconscious to create in physical reality.

Be careful to build the image of your perfect relationship, in general. **Don't limit the power of your subconscious by telling it that this relationship must be with any one certain person.** If the person you are with is the right one for you, the perfect relationship will develop. If another person is better for you, your subconscious will go to work to attract the situations that will allow you to meet and fall in love with this person.

Trust the infinite power of your mind; its connection with God, Spirit, or Infinite Intelligence; and your understanding of the situation. Don't get caught up in looking for "quick fixes" for problems that have taken years to develop. Know that your mind will be drawing upon infinite resources to create the situation that is best for you and release your limiting fixation with a specific result that you, in your current limited perception think is "right", so that your mind can create the result that is really best for you.

Lie #3: "I see things right"
This is the belief that the way you see things is the only way to see things or at least is the right way to see things. Nothing could be further from the truth.

Any physicist will now tell you that studies show that **matter and energy have no fixed, concrete existence. Matter is constantly changing into energy and energy is constantly changing into matter.**

This is shown in a basic way by Einstein's famous equation, $E=Mc^2$. This says that energy equals mass times the speed of light squared. According to this equation, energy and mass are exactly the same thing moving at different speeds or in different ways.

Since energy and mass are constantly changing, and everything we see is made up of energy and mass, the entire world around us is constantly changing. The only thing we can say for sure is that "This is how I perceive things." We cannot say, "This is how it is" for two reasons.

First, as you just learned, everything is changing constantly, so by the time we finish saying it, things will have changed.

Second, the way we think things are is determined by what we see in our world.

What we see on a physical level is limited by our faculty of sight. Our eyes perceive things at a rate of about 96 frames per four seconds. Horseflies' eyes register things at a much faster rate, and snails' eyes only focus at one frame every 4 seconds.

If we placed a book in front of a human, a horsefly, and a snail, and then moved it rapidly away, we would all perceive something different.

As a human, we would say that someone reached over and moved the book away. The motion would look relatively smooth to our eyes. The horsefly would see the whole thing as if there were gaps in the film because its eyes focus so much quicker than ours. And, since its eyes only focus on one frame every four seconds, the snail would argue all day (it probably doesn't have much else to do all day) that the book disappeared into thin air.

Which "view" would be "right"? All three are right for the particular person or thing doing the viewing.

The same is true about most of what we see around us. Even two relatively similar humans can have a totally different perception of the same exact thing. For example, if you and your best friend go to the forest and look at the trees, you might remember your first kiss in the soft sunlight filtering between the branches of the trees. You would think that the forest looked very friendly and inviting. Your friend, however, might remember how he got lost in the forest when he was a little kid and didn't think he'd ever see his mommy again. To him, the forest would look evil and uninviting.

Same forest. Same time. Totally different perception. And both perceptions are "right" for the person doing the perceiving.

"It is the commonest of mistakes to consider that the limit of our power of perception is also the limit of all there is to perceive." C.W. Leadbeater

There is no right and wrong when it comes to beauty, either. Beauty is based on perception as well. If we looked at a television screen under a microscope, we would see a bunch of flashing dots in all kinds of different colors. The changes in colors would look very random to us when we viewed the screen through the microscope. After a while, all their flashing and changing color might even begin to annoy us.

If, however, we took a step back and looked at the same screen from three our four feet away, we would see a beautiful lady with her trim body draped across our screen.

Same picture. Different perception. Both are "right."

The story of the stranger

Another good example of our limited perception is the story of a stranger walking down Main Street in a small town in the West. The grocer, whose store was on the east side of the street, and the banker, whose office was on the west side of the street, both saw the stranger pass through town.

Later that evening they were arguing about what color the man's hat was. The grocer insisted that it was blue and the banker argued that it was red.

Since both were convinced that they were right, they made a bet. The grocer bet all the inventory in his store that the man's hat was blue. The banker bet a two-foot pile of gold pieces that the man's hat was red.

The next day the man passed back through town from the other direction. As soon as he had passed, the grocer and the banker came charging out into the street and started accusing the other person of cheating.

The grocer had seen the man wearing a red hat and thought the banker had paid the stranger off to switch his hat to a red one that day. The banker had seen the man wearing a blue hat and insisted that the grocer had paid the stranger off to switch his red hat to a blue one that day.

Finally, they both looked at each other, looked down the street and took off running after the stranger to settle this dispute once and for all. When they caught up with the stranger, he just turned, smiled smugly, and tipped his hat to both sides. The grocer and the banker sheepishly turned and walked slowly back to town.

The man's cap had been red on one side and blue on the other. Both of their perceptions had been partially right.

Don't get caught in the two-colored hat trap. **Realize that your perception of the world is only partially correct. If it works for you, fine. Don't try to force it down others throats, because it may not work as well for them.** And, keep an experimental attitude that is always looking to understand the parts of "reality" that you currently do not perceive.

As Henry David Thoreau said in *Walden*, **"...If men would steadily observe realities only, and not allow themselves to be deluded, life... would be like a fairy tale...***we perceive that only* *great and worthy things have any permanent and absolute existence...Men establish and confirm their daily life of routine and habit everywhere, which still is built on purely illusory foundations.* **Children, who play life, discern its true law..."**

Remember, **you presently see the world as you are.** By uplifting who you are, you will understand better how things work and you will experience a new, higher, more peaceful level of life. That is the purpose of this book, so let's continue.

Lie #4: "I'm not responsible"

How many times have you heard this one? I'm not responsible for that. I couldn't help it. Things like that just happen.

What a bunch of crap.

<u>Things don't just happen. You can help it. And you are responsible.</u>

By this time, you probably know exactly why. You either choose the thoughts that enter your conscious mind or allow information, such as tv programs, to seep in. This data forms images in your subconscious and your subconscious dutifully goes to work to turn these images into physical reality. It triggers a set of emotions cause your actions, which in turn create your results.

Therefore, if you are reading this book, you are responsible for every single result in your life. ALL of them. Period.

Every result in our physical universe is a product of the thoughts of those of us that have inhabited it with our physical bodies. And we are perfectly capable of changing any result we don't like. All we have to do is choose new thoughts and build new images which will lead to new emotions and actions which will give us new results.

One of the most common areas where people attempt to brush off their own responsibility is in the area of wealth and money. Have you ever heard someone who a little (or a lot) short on cash say something like "It's not my fault. They laid me off" or "The economy sucks. No one can make money in an economy like this" or "I grew up poor and never had a chance" or "There's virtue in poverty." Have you ever said (or thought) anything like this?

All of these are examples of avoiding responsibility for the results in their lives, so let's just get right on with debunking these stupid myths right now. The fact is, if you got laid off, you weren't contributing more to the company than what they were paying you. Or the company heads are just stupid and didn't see your contribution.

If the first is true, get your head screwed on straight and realize that **no one owes you a living.** Why do you think we call it "earning" a living and not "getting" a living?

If you aren't contributing more than what someone is paying you, don't expect them to keep paying you. In fact, if you aren't contributing at least 10 times what they're paying you, you'll probably be looking for work soon because there are plenty of eager people out there who would be happy to contribute.

If the company heads are stupid and don't realize your contribution, you don't want to work for a company like that anyway. It's a waste of your life to spend your hours working for someone who doesn't appreciate your value. Go find a job elsewhere.

And don't tell me you can't do that.

We already discussed that issue earlier. You can find a job elsewhere. If you are really as good as you think you are, other companies will realize this and want to hire you. If they don't, maybe you should re-think how good you believe you are. Maybe you need to go out and improve

Stress-Free Success • 73

yourself and make yourself more valuable in the marketplace.

> People tell me all the time, "Well, I really want to work for THAT particular company" or "I don't want to move my family to take a new job elsewhere." That is fine, but don't complain about losing your job then because you just made a decision that you value working for THAT particular company or staying in THIS particular geographic location is more important than going out and taking advantage of a different opportunity.
>
> There's nothing wrong with that, but quit complaining about it because it's a choice YOU are making. Which means it's a choice you're free to change at any moment.

And don't forget, we live in America, the land of opportunity. We are all perfectly free to start our own business at any time. There are literally hundreds of legal, ethical, moral businesses you can start with little or no money or experience that can provide you with comfortable six-figure incomes in 3-7 years.

Don't believe me?

Ask any of the 1,000,000 plus people that have started some type of network marketing business in the last few years.

Now, how about the poverty is a virtue syndrome?

Get off that one, too.

Poverty is not a virtue.

As the Bible says, we are "created in the image and likeness of God." God has given us potential and it is our responsibility as humans to express that potential. To do anything less is to give up a part of our consciousness, which is what makes us uniquely human in the first place.

Money is a reward for service rendered. If you're not making much money, you must not be rendering much service. If you're not rendering much service, I doubt that you would argue that you're being very virtuous. Start viewing money as a vehicle for the expression of the goodness and potential inside of you and others.

There is nothing wrong with making money and being wealthy, if you use the money in a benevolent manner. You are a good person and will use your wealth for the good of mankind, so go for it. It's a heck of a lot more fun to be rich than poor. <u>And if you don't want the money for yourself, you'll have the fun and excitement of choosing exactly which cause you would like to donate it to.</u>

> So, eliminate the idea that other people are responsible for your life or the results you are getting in your life. Take responsibility for yourself.
>
> If you don't, no one else will, that's for sure.

You have incredible storehouses of potential locked away inside you. Once you find the keys that unlock this potential, you will be able to do things easily and naturally that you can hardly dream are possible right now. Studying and applying the ideas in this book and the natural laws that they describe is one of the keys to unlocking this potential.

Lie #5: "Others should do things the way I would"

This one screws people up all the time, too. **Others should not, and will not, do things the way you would, so don't expect them to.**

We are all unique expressions of the infinite Spirit. Each of us is the product of a different set of habits, beliefs, and conditioning. Our subconscious filters information in a different manner. Our feelings and emotions are different. We all perceive the world in a slightly different way. Therefore, <u>to expect others to act in the same way as we would in a situation is sheer folly. Don't do it.</u>

Each time you expect another person to act in a certain way, you are setting yourself up for disappointment. They will not see the situation in the same way you do, so they will not have the same feelings about the situation. Therefore, it's highly unlikely they would act in the same exact way you would. If you expect them to, you'll be disappointed virtually every time.

Trying to put others into a box that is just like yours is also a form of prejudice. Prejudice really is just pre-judging someone before you know the facts. If you expect someone to behave as you would, you are denying that person's individuality and you are definitely pre-judging the way you think they should behave, without knowing all the facts about their particular situation.

If we're talking virtue here, it's hardly virtuous to go around denying others individuality and assuming that you know better than they do how they should act.

Eliminate your expectations about others' behavior and practice *acceptance,* which is a form of true love. Accept them for who they are, and accept their actions for what they are, even if you don't agree with them.

This sends the message that you truly care about the other person as an individual and that you love the person that they are, independent of the individual actions that they take.

Eliminating expectations about others behavior from your life will also free up all kinds of psychic energy that you're now using to try to get people to act the way you want them to and to worry about it when they don't. You can re-invest all this new energy into productive, creative pursuits that will move your life further along the road to your dreams.

Lie #6: "I've spent too much to give it up now"
Almost all of us hold a deep-seeded belief that the time, effort, and money we spent in the past must be considered when making a decision in the present.

Not.

Expenditure of resources is only important *before* you expend them. You are not tied to a past mistake until you bind yourself to it. And you are the only one who can bind yourself to it.

The only thing you have today is the present value of an investment. Ask yourself, **"How can I make the most of this in the present and the future?"**

A few examples to illustrate:

About 80-90 percent of all individual stock market investors lose money because they are caught up in this trap. They hold on to loser stocks and watch them do down, down, down and then rationalize their decision by saying, "Some day it will go back up. If I sell it now, I'll lose the money I invested in it."

What they fail to realize is that their is no requirement that a stock every go back up and by holding on to "dogs" they are preventing themselves from ever making any money in the stock market.

What every successful stock market investor should do is continually ask, "What is the highest and best use of my money today? What is the best investment I can make with these dollars today?"

If that investment is different than the ones that are currently made, sell the current investments and buy the ones that are better (of course, don't go around doing this on a whim- make sure you know what a sound investment is before you start randomly selling stuff because you see "greener pastures" somewhere else).

The amount of money you originally invested is basically irrelevant in this decision. The only thing you have today is the current value of the investment, so it doesn't matter how much you paid for it. All that matters is whether or not that investment has bright prospects for making you money in the future. If it does, hold on. If it doesn't, sell it immediately and move on to something else with better potential.

The same is true for relationships.

Countless thousands of us rationalize our dead-end relationships daily with stupid logic like "I've got to make this work. I've invested too much time and energy in this to let it go now."

Get off it.

The amount of time and energy you've invested in the relationship in the past is totally irrelevant. It is totally impossible for you to live in the past and that's what that thought process is causing you to do. The only place you can ever live is the present, so live there.

Quit wasting your life holding on to the past.

Release it, NOW, before it's too late.

Go on with your life.

Ask yourself, "**Is this relationship one that I want today?** Do I feel healthy, vibrant, and positive about the relationship and the other person involved in it?" If the answer is yes, great. Enjoy every single moment of your wonderful relationship. **If the answer is no, move on.** You only live once and there is absolutely no reason to waste your life holding on to things you don't want and that aren't good for you j you've "invested too much to let them go."

Many of us hate to admit this because we have this subconscious belief that if we let this person go, we'll be lonely and won't ever find someone else. If you have ever thought that, remember two things.

First, **you don't NEED any other particular person in your life.** Relationships enhance life. They don't totally define life. You can do just fine without that person.

Second, **the only time you will be lonely is when you don't know yourself. Once you know yourself,**

you won't ever feel lonely again. You will have such a rich inner life that it won't bother you one iota to give up an unhealthy relationship because you will know that giving them up is like a good spring cleaning. It makes room for new, healthier relationships to come into your life.

And by all means **quit persecuting yourself for relationships that didn't work.** Every time you bother yourself with a relationship that didn't work, you're missing the beauty of the present moment because you're living in the past.

Remember, each present moment comes only once in your life and you can end up missing an awful lot of them real quick if you're not careful. Release the past. Don't judge it as good or bad.

It just was and that's it. You lived, you learned, and you're moving on to something better.

Never forget that.

Never forget that the time, energy, and money you have invested in something in the past means nothing when it comes to making decisions in the present.

Make your decisions from the clean slate of the present moment. Don't cloud them by hanging on to the past. The past is gone and you can't do a #%*&@! thing about it, so let it go. **View each moment as a blank page and decide exactly what's best for you and what will contribute most to living your ideal life in harmony with your mission and values. Then do it.** Joyously and without hesitation.

Lie #7: "I have the right to get that"

It is amazing how much time most of us waste running around trying to collect all the things we think we're entitled to. The fact of the matter is, **the ONLY thing we're entitled to is to choose our thoughts and our actions based on those thoughts so that we can express the fundamental goodness inside of us.**

<u>We are not entitled to jobs, to welfare, to group insurance, to workmen's comp, or any of the other myriad things we waste billions of dollars and hours every year trying to collect.</u>

Everything other than our fundamental right to choose our thoughts and actions we either earn or we enjoy as a by-product of choosing to live in the society that we do.

We <u>earn</u> our job. We <u>earn</u> our income. We <u>earn</u> the money to pay for insurance. We enjoy good roads, clean restrooms, clear telecommunications, efficient sewage, and other benefits because we have chosen to live in modern American society. These things are privileges that we earn through our contribution to society. They are not rights that we are entitled to for doing nothing.

Learn to appreciate the abundance around you. Invest your resources in improving yourself, setting an example for others, and building a bright future for you and those that come after you.

Don't waste your time and money trying to collect "rights" that are really privileges.

Remember, you are perfectly free to live anywhere you choose. If your neighborhood doesn't give you what you want, move.

If you aren't happy with what you get as a member of American society, move. If you can't afford insurance or other benefits on your income, figure out a way to increase your income. Start a business on the side. Work part-time on weekends. Educate yourself so you can earn more per hour.

If the people around you don't want to do what you want to do or aren't taking the actions you would like them to take, move on. You are free to choose who you associate with.

If a certain mind-set or type of action is that important to you, find others who think, believe, and act the same way you do and spend your time with them. It's much more productive and you'll be much happier than hanging around people you don't like and complaining that they're doing it all wrong or don't believe the way you do.

Don't waste your life trying to collect all these rights you think you're entitled to. **Since someone else will always control what you "get" when you try to "collect," you're going to be throwing your life away worrying about what they arbitrarily decided to give you.** Wouldn't it make more sense to take the positive approach of pursuing your dreams so that you can have anything you want?

The 5 biggest lies about your happiness that you probably believe right now...

L:ie #1: "He (or she) makes me happy"
This is one of the biggest myths screwing up our society today. **Other people do not make you happy, no matter who they are. YOU make YOURSELF happy.**

Period.

Happiness is not an external event that other people can turn on or off, like a faucet. Happiness comes from within. It is a choice you make moment by moment. Every second of every day, no matter who you are with or who you are not with, you have the choice. You can be happy or you can be unhappy.

Why not choose happiness?

If we persist in thinking that other people make us happy, we're going to have this uneasy feeling of insecurity gnawing away inside of us all of the time. If they make us happy, then it would also follow that we'd probably be unhappy (or not as happy), when we're not around them.

This is especially true with love relationships. We think of the other person as our source of happiness and then we become dependent on them for our happiness. If we think our marriage partner makes us happy, then we become dependent on them for our happiness and lose sight of the goodness inside of ourselves. Since we are building an illusion that happiness comes from an external source, we always feel insecure because we think they have the power to pull the rug from under us and jerk our happiness away. *They only have that power if WE give them that power.*

Our happiness and our unhappiness comes solely from our <u>reactions</u> to people and things. We are completely free to react to them in any way that we choose.

Begin viewing others as enhancements to your happiness and people to share your happiness with, not as the source of your happiness. Play with this idea and see if it doesn't make a big difference in your outlook on life and relationships.

Take responsibility for yourself. Start telling yourself that **you are the one who makes you happy or unhappy, and that you are choosing in this very moment to be happy, regardless of who is or isn't around you and regardless of how those who are around you are responding to you.**

Since the only thing that cannot be taken away from you is your mind, it is also the only thing that can give you any sense of security and peace. Look inside yourself for your happiness. Realize that you are a beautiful expression of infinite spirit and you have plenty of goodness inside of you.

The converse of this paradigm is also false. **Other people do not make you unhappy, either. It's your reactions to them or their actions that create your unhappiness and you are free to choose not to react negatively at any time.** If you go around saying, "He upset me" or "She shouldn't do that to me" or "I don't deserve to be treated like that," you are giving others power to control you through the way that they respond to you.

Is that something you want to give them?

Probably not, unless you enjoy being a <u>dependent little clod of pathetic problems</u>.

Quit thinking that they should respond to you in a certain way.

Quit thinking that you must respond to them in a certain way.

There is nothing saying you should be upset when someone insults you. You're free to brush it off and smile right back at them. The only reason they were insulting you is because they had an insecure need to feel superior. Don't give them what they want by getting angry about it. Ignore the insult and go on with your life. Sooner or later, they'll get the picture that insulting you doesn't bother you, and it won't get them the attention that they crave.

Translated, that means they'll quit the needless insults, and in the meantime, you'll be leading a much happier life.

Try it.

Lie #2: "Material wealth will make me happy"

This one is really messing up a lot of our lives. As we just discussed, happiness comes from within you. It is a choice you make on a moment-by-moment basis. At any point in time, you can choose to be happy, no matter how little money you may have.

There are thousands of happy, poor people in the world. And thousands of unhappy wealthy people. It isn't the money, or lack of it, that makes them happy or unhappy. It is how they respond to life and the choice that they make about how to perceive the world around them that creates their happiness or unhappiness.

Many of us are wasting large chunks of our lives running around trying to accumulate material wealth because we think it will make us happy.

It won't.

We work 70 hours a week at a job we hate just to earn money to pay for the car to drive to work in and the house that we enjoy for about 15 minutes each evening before we crash from exhaustion.

And we repeat this pattern, day in, day out for years.

In my dictionary, that matches the definition of "stupid" very well.

But let's take it a step further.

Let's assume this pattern goes on for years. Finally, it starts to "pay off." We begin getting raises, moving up the ladder. Our business starts cranking and we're earning all kinds of money. We buy the BMW, the big house in suburbia, and take our family on vacations to Europe each summer. <u>We're living the "American dream" but we don't feel happy.</u>

Why?

<u>We just invested tens of thousands of hours accumulating material wealth and material wealth does not make us happy.</u> We make ourselves happy.

What has probably happened is that we've been so focused on creating material wealth, we've neglected to create any inner emotional and spiritual wealth for ourselves. We are out of balance. Our feeling of unhappiness is a sign that our inner being is in conflict with the outer person we are trying to act like. If this is you, slow down and think about your life. If you had one week left to live, how would you spend it? Would it matter how much material wealth you had?

Don't make the mistake, though, of thinking that material wealth is bad.

It is not.

In fact, it is very good.

The material things that we buy and create are expressions of our creativity and our individuality. They allow us to enjoy life more fully. And, our purchases keep

Stress-Free Success • 84

money circulating, which allows others to enjoy their lives more fully as they earn livings for themselves.

But the material wealth itself doesn't make us happy.

Lie #3: "Once I get that, I'll be happy"

Hold your horses.

Think about this for a second.

Is it possible to live in the past?

No.

Is it possible to live in the future? No.

The ONLY time you can ever live in is the present.

If you make your happiness dependent on some future event, you are sacrificing the present for some unknown future. Since the present is the only time you can ever live in, what you are really doing is sacrificing your life, period.

Don't do it.

Postponed happiness is lost happiness.

If you have ever told yourself, "Once I get some money (or a new lover or a new house or whatever it was), I'll be happy," I would almost guarantee that you also sometimes feel like a gerbil on one of those funny wheel contraptions that we put in their cages. The faster you run, the more worn out you get, but you don't get any closer to your happiness.

Why?

Happiness is not a future event. It can only be enjoyed NOW. Now is the only time you'll ever have, so don't waste it. <u>Enjoy all your present moments because that is all you'll ever have.</u>

Live your life with the attitude that "My life is unfolding perfectly for me. I am living 100% and enjoying each one of my present moments for what they are."

And don't forget **happiness comes from within. You are perfectly free to choose to be happy, no matter what the circumstances are around you.**

It's your life.

Choose happiness.

Give up making yourself unhappy.

One of the biggest lies that we've been sold is that things or other people make us happy. They don't. Period.

ALL happiness is in your own mind. It comes from deep inside of you and nowhere else.

If you think your marriage partner (or anyone else) makes you happy, then you have to keep them around to be happy. This makes you dependent on them for your happiness. It <u>steals your freedom</u> to be the person you really are and express yourself fully. You are always scared and insecure inside because you know that if they have the power to make you happy, they also have the power to take your happiness away. This is a <u>severe form of dependency</u>. Don't get caught up in it.

It's like trying to walk across a pond on thin ice. You'll never be relaxed. You may take a few steps forward, but eventually you're going to fall through and get all cold inside from the icy water below.

Remember, YOU make yourself happy. No other person or external thing can ever make you happy. Other people and external things can add to your enjoyment of life. They can be vehicles for helping you express the happiness that is already inside of you. But they cannot MAKE you happy in and of themselves.

Don't try to put square pegs in round holes by looking to external things for your happiness. Look inside yourself. Not only will you find an incredible reservoir of goodness just waiting to be tapped, you will have the peace of mind of knowing that your reservoir has an infinite supply of happiness that can never be taken away from you.

Lie #4: "If I sacrifice today, I'll be happy tomorrow"

Sacrifice. The word has been almost deified in our screwed up society.

We are programmed to think that sacrifice is good and that if we're not sacrificing, we're somehow not quite as good as someone else who is.

What's really happening is a select group of those who hold power in the organizations that you belong to are feeding you this line so that they can maintain their power. They know that if you think you must sacrifice to be a good person and you want to be a good person, they can get you to do things you otherwise wouldn't do by calling them a "sacrifice" in the name of goodness.

Now, you're probably saying, <u>if I didn't sacrifice anything, I'd be living a selfish, hedonistic lifestyle that wouldn't be doing me or anyone else any good. That may be true. But it may not.</u>

If you insist on sacrificing something, sacrifice everything that does not move you closer to your goals; sacrifice everything that does not fit with YOUR values (not the values of those around you); sacrifice every task and responsibility that does not help you to unfold the incredible goodness inside of you; and by all means sacrifice the necessity to live up to others' standards and do what they tell you is "good."

Good is not an absolute. You must decide for yourself what is good and bad. If your standard of good does not agree with the standard of your church or government or friends, you are perfectly free to choose your surroundings. You can join a new church; you can move to a different city or country; and you can make new friends.

The choice is yours.

The question to ask yourself is **"Would I do this thing anyway or am I only doing it because someone else told me I 'should' suffer through it in the name of goodness and a better tomorrow?"**

If you are only doing it because someone fed you the line that it would create a better 'tomorrow', <u>you are falling prey to the infamous 'nebulous future' trap</u>.

How many politicians have been elected through this very same method? They tell you that if you do what they want, they will help you get something you want, 'sometime in the nebulous future.'

Does it work?

How many politicians do you know who have given you everything they promised after they were elected?

I thought so...

<u>Remember, you can only live in the present. There is absolutely no way to live in the past or the future. The present is all you've got and if you sacrifice it, you're sacrificing the only thing you've got.</u>

Is it worth it?

I highly doubt it.

Suffering today to enjoy something 'better' tomorrow is like throwing yourself overboard to feel the relief of being rescued.

It's just not necessary.

You can fully enjoy today without sacrificing and without suffering.

How?

Examine your decisions from the perspective of how they fit into your goals, values and beliefs. Sacrifice and suffering only occur when you are doing things that go against the grain of your natural being.

<u>Be like a stream. Let your life flow smoothly and naturally. When you reach a rocky point, don't stop to bang your head against it. Just let yourself flow right on past it.</u> Soon you will flow around a bend and the rocks will be out of sight.

If the action fits into your goals, values, and beliefs, do it. It is no longer a sacrifice. It is just a step along the path to a better life.

For example, imagine that you highly value your health, believe that working out is an important way to improve your health, and have set a goal of lowering your body fat by 4% by the end of the year. To go out and do your daily half-hour jog is not a sacrifice. Even when you are panting and your muscles are burning, you are not sacrificing because you are moving forward toward your goal. You feel pain but you do not suffer because you know that you are growing and improving.

As John Mellencamp aptly put it, "**It hurts so good.**"

One more common example before we move on:

> *Often I talk to salespeople who seem to feel that they are sacrificing their lives in order to go out on sales calls to make a little money. If that is you, quit right now.*

If you don't enjoy what you're doing, don't do it.

Happiness is in the process, not the end goal. If you don't enjoy the cruise down the road to your goal, you will not enjoy your destination. Instead, you will reach your goal and come up with a feeling of emptiness inside. This is because you were sacrificing. You were wasting your present moments in a game you didn't like.

This is what we mean by the **difference between achieving goals and living your values**. There is an important distinction. If you keep your values in front of you at all times, you can achieve your goals AND live your values.

This will give you a profound sense of inner satisfaction. Yes, there will be struggles and challenges along the way, but you will view them with joy as a part of becoming the person you need to be to achieve your goals.

If you rush around going after goals that don't match your values, you will always have a sense of dissatisfaction inside, no matter how many goals you accomplish. You will know that you are sacrificing, and your body and mind will tell you that this is wrong. Their message will show up in headaches, colds, flu, heart disease, irritability, pain, regret, grief, and a lack of inner peace.

If selling your product or service seems like a pain or something you do only to make money, find something else to do immediately. <u>You are sacrificing the only life you have to live for some future 'happiness' that will never arrive.</u>

If, however, you truly believe in and enjoy selling your product or service, you will know that the long hours you put in and thousands of miles you travel are not sacrifices. They are just steps along the way to accomplishing your unique mission in life. You will work and travel with joy in your heart, knowing that you are privileged to be able to touch lives and help others with the product or service that you sell.

The point is, sacrifice is a relative term. What is a sacrifice to one person is a privilege to another. That's why some people thoroughly enjoy the often harsh life of a Peace Corps worker in Africa or the intense lifestyle of a paramedic.

They are living in the present moment and doing those things that they believe in and value.

This isn't sacrifice. It's happiness.

Now, back to how you can live your life without sacrifice and without suffering. All you have to do is follow one simple rule: **if it matches your beliefs, values, and goals, it is not a sacrifice.**

Do it.

And enjoy yourself fully.

If it conflicts with your beliefs, values, and goals, it's a sacrifice. Don't do it.

And don't feel guilty or persecute yourself for not doing it. Just joyously invest your time in something else that does match your beliefs, values, and goals. After all, it's your life and you only live it once. By making decisions in this way, you are helping all those around you by serving as a shining example of a human life *lived with integrity and honesty*.

Lie #5: "Suffering makes me a more noble, more pure person"

Wrong. Period.

> ***Get off the martyr kick.*** *Most people who go around saying they are suffering to become better people are really just telegraphing their insecurity about themselves. They know that suffering will draw attention to themselves and they crave attention, so they act like they're suffering.*
>
> *Often, they also have low self-esteems and subconsciously think, "There's something wrong with me. I'm not as good as other people. I don't really deserve to be happy." So they suffer needlessly.*

Or their lack of confidence makes them afraid to stand out in a crowd. They know that if they succeed and reach high and lofty goals, they will be in the small minority. They know that others will probably be jealous and make fun of them. They won't be part of the "in crowd" at the bowling alley or the poker table anymore. Heaven forbid that they would actually break free of their chains and make something of their life.

That would mean taking responsibility for themselves and not blaming others for everything that happened to them.

Oh no, what a terrible burden to bear.

How could they ever stand to not make excuses for everything in their lives? And what would they ever do if their old "friends" teased them about being successful?

"Total stress. Can't handle it. Gotta stay part of the pathetic clod of ailments called the masses. Can't stand out."

And so they suffer.

Then they go home from the bowling alley and poker game and their family rubs it in some more. Who gets all the attention in the family? The one who complains the most and seems to be "suffering" the most. Who does everyone say is a good, generous person? The ones who give up all their dreams and quit being their own person, so they can spend their entire life doing things for other people.

The family doesn't realize that **people who ignore themselves and try to seem like they're doing everything for everybody else are really the most selfish of all**. Their low self-esteem means that they need compliments to boost their ego and they need the attention that their deeds bring to them.

The families fail to realize that the greatest people are those who make their own lives an example of personal excellence. Who develop themselves to the point where they have incredible reservoirs of love and kindness to give to others unselfishly because this giving is done by choice and not by the necessity of gaining attention or a boost to their self-esteem.

Yes, our families and friends often fail to realize all this. So they continue glorifying the martyrs.

And we continue to suffer, because we think that is what is right.

But it's not right.

There's no need to run around being a martyr. **Get off your tail and go out and do something productive with your life. Quit whining and complaining just so people feel sorry for what a truly pathetic life you live.** The truth is, there are millions of people living much tougher lives. Just ask the natives in Botswana or the slums of India and you'll see that your life is blessed with amazing prosperity in comparison to theirs.

> *What do you really want to do with your life? What are your dreams and goals and passions? Build the image of you succeeding at them in your mind. Burn it into your subconscious until its flame burns so bright that the laughter of your jealous friends no longer bothers you and the comfort of the attention your martyrdom brings no longer interests you. Take responsibility for yourself. Go forth boldly with your torch held high before you. Dare to succeed. Dare to make something beautiful out of your life.*

You are a creative expression of Infinite Spirit. Spirit is always for expansion. Whining, complaining, and suffering to draw attention to you is NOT expanding. These things go against the highest part of your being. **Don't fight your spiritual nature. Allow the greatness inside of you to flow out and bless the world.** Take responsibility for yourself and lead a happy life of prosperity and abundance. That is what being a good, noble person is really all about.

Money lies, money lies, and more money lies....
why we aren't as wealthy as we could be today

Why aren't you wealthy today?

The major reason most of us aren't financially independent today is that we are laboring under a false paradigm of wealth. Our beliefs about money are holding us back from creating the prosperity that we deserve.

Understanding what money is, now it works, what it is good for (and what it isn't good for) will allow us to create a wealth paradigm that works better for us.

The first thing we need to understand is what money is. **Money is a symbol of energy.** It is a convenient way to trade goods and services. I find it much more convenient to carry around a hundred bucks than a sack full of my books. I'd bet that Lee Iacocca would say the same thing about carrying around a trailer full of Chryslers.

Money represents the value that we place on various goods or services. Since it is a symbol, it has no value in and of itself. Its only value is that which we assign to it.

Since God or spirit is always for expansion, money is a symbol of this expansion. You can view money as a reward that you receive for service rendered. It is like receiving a plaque for being employee of the month, except that when you receive money, you can go out and trade it for other things you would like instead of just hanging it on your wall.

> Think of all the good that money can do in the work. As Russell Conwell said, **"Money printed your Bible, money building your churches, money sends your missionaries, and money pays your preachers, and you would not have many of them, either, if you did not pay them."**

Keeping the role of money in perspective will help free you from any negative thought patterns regarding wealth. **Earn money joyously and never feel guilty for the money you earn.** At the same time, don't let money rule your life.

Take the words of P.T. Barnum to heart, "**Money is a terrible master but an excellent servant.**" Think of money as a servant that will do your bidding. It is up to you as master to take responsibility for giving your servant orders to do good.

The 7 biggest lies that are keeping you from being truly wealthy...

Lie #1: "I want (or need) money"

You do not want or need money.

Period.

You want or need the things that you can use money to buy.

Imagine you being hungry. You can't eat because you have no money. You are walking dejectedly down the street when out of the blue, a stranger appears and offers you a million dollars. Your eyes light up and you follow him to where the money is located. He ushers you into a room full of cash. The room is piled high with wads of green backs.

You're in heaven until you hear the door shut and lock behind you. You look around and realize that you now have more money that you could hardly imagine but you still can't eat, because you're locked in a room with no food. What you wanted was the food, not the money.

Keep this in mind as you go through your day. **You really want what money can buy, not the money itself.** Money is a direct way to get the things you want, but it is not the only way. If you could trade your services for what you want directly or could create some other means of getting it, you would be just as satisfied as if you bought it with money.

Therefore, don't get caught up in making money just to be making money. You don't want the money, anyway, and money is only a symbol. It has no intrinsic value. Always remember that there is a way to receive anything you want into your life. All you have to do is become aware of it. Money may or may not be involved.

Lie #2: "I don't have enough money to do that"

If you believe this, you are right.

However, if you don't believe it, you are also right.

Why?

Once you tell your subconscious mind that you don't have enough money to do something, you are setting up an image of lack. Your subconscious, ever your faithful servant, then goes to work to turn this image of lack into physical reality.

What happens?

Presto.

It finds a way to make sure that you don't have enough money to do that.

When you are in a situation where your current finances would not allow you to do what you would like, come at the situation from the opposite angle.

For example, if you want to go on a cruise at the end of the year but you don't think you'll have enough money to do it, tell yourself that "I am prosperous and all the money I need is flowing to me on a daily basis."

Build an image in your mind of you experiencing the cruise - the sun beating down on your bronzed skin, romantic sunsets from the edge of the ship, playing games all day, dancing all night, eating the best food in the world and as much of it as you would like. Become emotionally involved with this picture and turn it over to your subconscious and relax. Let your subconscious do its work. It will attract the resources that you need to take your trip in ways that you will never be able to predict in advance.

Trust yourself and trust the power of the universe around you. But don't expect to have a bunch of money flowing in for doing nothing. Your subconscious will provide you with cues for the actions that you must take. Follow your instincts and take these actions and you will create the prosperity that you desire and deserve.

Lie #3: "It takes money to make money"
This is a common myth that has no facts to support it. **There are two ways to make money - people at work or money at work.** That means, if you don't have money to put to work, you can always put people to work. Those people may include yourself, but they certainly don't have to .

There is **one key that unlocks the power of wealth multiplication, whether you decide to put money to work or people to work. That key is IDEAS.** You see, the **only thing that it really takes to make money is a good idea.** And the idea doesn't even have to be yours. Burger King was not a new idea. It was just a take-off of a successful concept that McDonald's pioneered.

Remember these key points:

1. First, **there is always a way.** Every time you have a desire it is a sign of an unfulfilled potentiality inside of you. You do not get true desires that cannot be fulfilled, so if you truly desire to be wealthy, you can do it. **The way already exists. All you have to is become aware of it.**

2. Second, remember, **all it takes is one good idea acted upon and you'll be set for life.** Bill Gates at Microsoft, Rich Devos and Jay Van Andel at Amway, Tom Onaghan of Domino's Pizza fame, and Ray Kroc, king of the McDonald's golden arches, all had one good idea that they acted upon. That was all it took to make them some of the wealthiest people in the world, and that's all it will take to make you financially independent for life. Even if you're starting with no money today.

3. Third, **don't overlook the wealth in your own backyard.** The way for you to become wealthy is usually right under your nose.

> In Russell Conwell's famous speech, "Acres of Diamonds," he tells the story of an old Persian farmer named Al Hafed. Al Hafed was eaking out an average existence for he and his family when one day an ancient Buddhist priest, one of the wise men of the East, visited him.
>
> They got to talking and the priest told Al Hafed the story of how the world was created. He told him how when the earth was formed, different parts of the molten mass cooled at different rates. The parts that cooled the slowest of all became the hardest substance known to man - diamonds. The priest told him that if he had a diamond the size of his thumb nail, he could purchase a dozen farms like his.
>
> And with a handful of diamonds, he could become one of the wealthiest men in the country. All Hafed's eyes lit up. He went to bed dreaming of his own mine of diamonds.
>
> When he woke up, he sought the priest and asked him where diamonds were found. The priest told him that if he wanted diamonds, he would have to find a stream of water that runs over white sands, between high mountains. In the white sands, the priest said, Al Hafed would find the diamonds he sought.
>
> Al Hafed sold his farm, left his family and relatives and went off in search of diamonds. He searched across Palestine, through Europe, and finally he wandered into Barcelona, Spain. By this time, he was starving and the only thing he owned was the few rags he wore. Poor Al Hafed could not resist the temptation to throw himself into a tidal wave between the

pillars of Hercules in one last attempt to find his diamonds. He sank beneath its foaming crest, never to rise in this life again.

The man who purchased Al Hafed's farm let his camel out to drink one day. When the camel puts its head in the water, the man noticed a flash of light from the white sands of the stream. He reached down and picked up a dark stone with a strange eye of light. He put it on his mantel and forgot about it.

The old priest returned one day and saw the stone. He was shocked. "Here is a diamond! Has Al Hafed returned? The new owner of the farm told him it wasn't a diamond, but a stone he found out in the garden. The priest would not believe him. They rushed out to the garden and began digging in the sand. They found other finer specimens and discovered the diamond mines of Golconda, the richest diamond mines in the history of the world.

Yes, literally acres of diamonds were right in Al Hafed's backyard. If only he had stayed home and mined the diamonds he already had, he would have been one of the wealthiest men in history.

Don't forget your acres of diamonds. We all have them and we can all become wealthy by mining them.

Lie #4: "I'm not smart enough to become wealthy"

That's a bunch of bull. Many of the wealthiest people in the world never finished school and some of the most "educated" ones, those academics with a whole wall full of degrees, are barely making ends meet. **The truth is, it doesn't take great brains to become wealthy. All it take is one simple idea acted upon and stuck with until it works.**

Think about it.

Did it take a rocket scientist to invent a hamburger or a pizza or a pair of jeans?

Hardly.

Yet, Ray Kroc, Tom Monaghan, and Levi Strauss all became rich and famous for figuring out what to do with these simple inventions. Learn from these great men.

You see, **the greatest mind is always the simplest..** The greatest inventors are those that see some simple need and then invent something to fill that need. They know the eternal truth that if they come up with need, there are other people out there who need it, too.

The only thing you need to do to become wealthy is find out what people WANT (not need) to buy and then sell it to them. It's that simple.

You don't have to beat your head on the wall trying to come up with some new, high-tech gadget or whizbang invention. Keep it simple.

Look around you every day and you will see all kinds of <u>wants</u> that you could fill. That's what the inventors of Leggs pantyhose did. And the founders of the great motel chains that realized weary travelers wanted safe, clean places to sleep. And the original fast food kings who realized that the accelerating pace of American life would mean that we would be eating out much more often than we ever did before.

Pick one need that get you excited and figure out a way to fill it. You can do that no matter what your supposed IQ or education *level, so get started today.*

Lie #5: "Money is evil"

Here's one of the most common myths that holds people back from ever achieving financial security. How many times have you heard people tell you that the Bible says money is evil? If anyone has ever told you that, tell them to go back and read their Bible.

The Bible says, "The love of money is evil" Money itself is not evil. *Get out a dollar bill and look at it closely right now. Is there anything about it that looks evil to you? Unless you're a kind of screwed up freak, I really doubt you could find anything evil about a piece of paper with some green ink on it. It's not the money itself that is evil. It's what you do with it that could be evil, if it is not used properly.*

Used properly, however, money is a faithful servant that will allow you to do all kinds of good in the world. You can have all the good intentions in the world, but it there isn't money involved somewhere, it's going to be difficult to accomplish many of your goals, no matter how altruistic they are.

Remember the story of the Good Samaritan. He would never have been remembered for good intentions. He had money and put his money to good use. For that he is remembered and revered 2000 year later. The same is true for the religious leaders of today. Without money, we could not create missions or program to help the homeless, cripple, or needy. We could not feed starving children in Third World nations and we would have almost no museums and orchestras to enjoy. Not to mention that without money, we would probably have no clothes on our backs, no roof over our heads, no car to drive, no hot food to eat, and no warm bed to sleep in. If that sounds good to you, keep thinking that money is evil. You'll end up with a life lacking all those things.

As for me, I'll take the high road" and choose prosperity in my life - along with the clothing, shelter, food, bed and opportunity to help others that money will bring.

Eliminate the idea that money is evil from your mind. Begin telling yourself that "Money is my friend. It is an obedient servant that will do whatever I ask of it. As a faithful and moral master, I will only ask money, my servant, to perform duties that benefit myself and all of mankind." That is a prosperous, healthy attitude about money.

Cultivate this attitude by always asking yourself, **"What good things will I do with the money I am attracting into my life? How will this money help myself and others lead happier, more fulfilling lives?"**

Lie #6: "Only dishonest or bad people are rich"

People hold this false belief for two reasons. First, they fall prey to their lens of perception. In other words, they find exactly what they're looking for.

If you look for dishonest or bad people with money, guess what you'll find?

Dishonest or bad people with money.

No peace of mind, I guarantee, but they'll have money nonetheless.

If you look for honest, generous, good people with lots of money, guess what you'll find?

Honest, generous, good people with lots of money.

There are plenty of them out there. I know, because at a very early age I began developing the belief that it is possible to earn lots of money without compromising your morals or beliefs. The stronger this belief became in my mind, the more examples I found to support this belief. I began attracting wealthy, generous people into my life.

Not only did I meet these people, I became friends and even business partners with them. Because that's exactly what I was looking for. The same thing will happen to you.

The law of attraction states that you will attract that which you are and that which you are looking for. Invest in yourself and you will become capable of attracting prosperous, generous people into your life. It is true that birds of a feather flock together so become part of the honest, wealthy flock.

And **be sure to make your glass half full, not half empty.** Each time you focus on prosperity, you will find it everywhere around you.

Lie #7: "Making money will solve my problems"

If you think money will solve your problems, I feel sorry for you. You are going to have a ton of problems that rest of your life.

The truth about problems is they cannot be solved on the same level they are created. Read that again. A problem cannot be solved on the same level that it is created. <u>The way to solve problems is to raise yourself to a level above the problem</u>. Then, the problem either dissipates of its own accord (most do) or you will become aware of the solution to the problem.

Throwing money at problems never solves them. It may slow them down in the short term, but that's about it. Imagine your problem as a cut on your finger. You place a bandage over it. The bandage temporarily "solves" the problem, but unless the wound underneath heals, the cut will still be there when you take the bandage off. Throwing money at the problem works the same way. The money is like the bandage for the cut. It may seem to solve the problem, but all it is really doing is temporarily covering it up. It is doing nothing for healing the real cause of the problem.

Become aware that **the source of <u>all</u> your problems is your own mind.** Your own mind creates your problems by determining how you react to situations.

The Great Law of your being states that energy just is. It is not inherently good or bad. Since each situation in your life is a manifestation of energy in different forms, the situation itself is not inherently good or bad. It is totally neutral and you can decide how you want to react to it.

In North America, we would be appalled if our son came home with a skull on his spear from a fellow human he had just beheaded. Until a few years ago, if we were living in Borneo, we would be appalled if our son did NOT come home with a few skulls. Beheading a couple of enemies was a sign of manhood and it was a disgrace for a young warrior to not follow the rites of manhood.

The situation was exactly the same. Our conditioning caused us to react to it in a totally different way. The same is true of every situation we face in our lives. We are always free to react to the situation in any way we choose. We can choose to perceive the situation as good or bad, and we can change our conditioning so that our desired reactions become natural.

As you can see, all of the conditioning that determines how we naturally react to a situation as well as the thoughts that we use to change that conditioning originate in our minds. **It is inside our own minds that our problems start.**

To really solve them, we must address them on a level that is at least as high as the level on which they are created. Since our mind functions on the intellectual and universal/spiritual level, we must solve our problems on this level. Throwing money at a problem is trying to solve the problem on the lower, physical level. It cannot be done successfully on a permanent basis.

Most people misunderstand this. When they have inner feelings of insecurity or low self-esteem, they go out and buy new clothes or cars or other "toys" to try to replace their feeling of emptiness. This is why so many so-called rich people are unhappy. They scrambled their entire life to make money, thinking lots of money would solve the problems inside of them. Then, they got the money and it didn't solve a single problem.

When people are standing in unemployment lines because they are not educated enough to find a decent job or because they have a set of conditioning that is preventing them from holding a permanent job, we give them money and then wonder why they are back in the unemployment line a few weeks later. Their problem is mental/spiritual and we are trying to solve it on a physical level. It doesn't work.

When we don't have enough money to pay our bills, we blame our employer for not paying us enough or the slow economy for preventing us from getting a job. We think more money will solve the problem. It won't. It will temporarily cover it but unless we change what's in our minds, the problem will occur again regularly.

The problem is in our own minds. If we were aware of how to create more value, we could have any job we wanted. It we were aware of what businesses thrive in a down economy, we would look into those industries. No matter what laws are passed or what shape the economy is in, some people make money and others lose it.

Why?

Those that are truly wealthy understand that money is a symbol for the exchange of energy. They understand the laws governing the creation of wealth and follow these laws. They do not try to use money as a bandage for their mental and emotional problems.

Quit looking to money as a cure for your problems and quit blaming lack of money as a cause for your problems. Doing either sets up a blockage inside of you that will prevent you from ever becoming wealthy. Instead, realize that money is a reward for service rendered.

Figure out how to render more service and you will naturally earn more money. Realize that your problems cannot be solved on a lower level than the one on which they are created. Address your problems at their source - your own mind. Raise your level of awareness so that your problems will dissipate or you will become aware of a simple, natural solution to them.

A simple way to start doing this is to ask, "**What's right about this situation? How could I choose to**

react more positively to this situation? Will my negative reaction actually improve the situation or will it just cause me stress"?

Then **try not reacting to a situation at all.**

Just stay neutral and observe it.

Since your reactions come entirely from your own mind, you are perfectly free to choose not to react.

Tell yourself, "I am choosing not to react to this situation. I realize that the situation is not negative unless I make it negative and I am choosing not to make it negative. I am observing what is happening without reacting."

Experiment with that attitude. It will pay big dividends in your life and soon you will be freeing all kinds of negative psychic energy that you have had tied up in reacting to all the situations going on around you. You'll be able to reinvest all this extra energy into creating positive, prosperous relationships and wealthy, abundant lifestyle.

Won't that be a wonderful reward just for choosing not to react negatively to the situations around you?

A FREE GIFT FOR YOU before we move on:
I've found that it often takes a while to eliminate the effects of believing in the lies we've discussed in this chapter. To help you move smoothly through this step toward Stress-Free Success, I've prepared a **Special Report titled, "Stress-Free Success: Phase Two."** *This Special Report takes you beyond the ideas you've learned in this book and gives you the strategies you need to move to the next level where you are integrating the ideas effortlessly into your life and watching your stress quickly melt away. Normally, this Special Report is $10, but as a reader of this book, I'm offering it to you* **FREE**, *as my gift to you. I do ask, however, that you cover the $3 for shipping and handling to get the report to you. A form for requesting your FREE Report is at the back of this book.*

Lesson 8:
Harness GOAL POWER To Multiply Your Success Without Stress

Now we are ready to move on to the "good stuff" - setting and achieving goals that will allow you to live your ideal life. In the next few chapters, you will learn a process that has helped thousands of people around the world turn their dreams into reality. It can do the same for you, <u>if you follow each step in order and don't try to skip anything or shortcut the system.</u>

Remember, goal achievement is a scientific process, and processes only work if you do.

The sad truth about goals

The sad truth about goals is that most of us have none. A study by Success Motivation Institute found that 97 percent of people never set any goals at all. They just drift through life without any real direction. The 3 percent of people who do set goals accomplish more than the other 97 percent combined.

Sadly, <u>most of us spend more time planning our Christmas party than we do planning our lives.</u> We spend more hours in front of the television in one month than the hours we invest in setting and achieving goals during our entire lifetime. As **Denis Waitley** says about most Americans in *Seeds of Greatness*, "They squander their money, their time, and their minds with activities that are 'tension-relieving' instead of 'goal-achieving.'"

> The results of this total lack of concern for realizing our potential and expressing our talents are even sadder. According to the U.S. Department of Labor, only three out of every hundred Americans are financially independent when they reach age 65. The other 97 must

depend on relatives and their monthly Social Security checks just to survive.

We cannot blame this pathetic statistic on lack of income or job opportunity, either. Even in the high-income professions such as medicine and law, only five out of every hundred people are financially independent at age 65. And that's after 40 years of earning some of the highest incomes in the country.

What is the problem here?

Obviously, most of us have no idea how to manage money. Just as importantly, though, most of us have no plan for managing our money. <u>It is the lack of a simple, executable plan that holds us back from achieving the financial prosperity we all deserve.</u>

The same concept holds true for the rest of our lives. **We wouldn't think of trying to build a house without a blueprint, but virtually all of us try to build a successful life without a plan.**

In this section, you will begin to understand what goals really are, why they are important, and how the goal achievement process works. Then you will learn exactly how to choose a proper goal and <u>how to develop a plan</u> that will guarantee that you will be one of the few that achieves your goals and lives a life of true splendor and abundance.

What is a goal?

Before you can begin setting and achieving your goals, you need to know what a goal really is.

Take a minute and finish this sentence: **"To me, a goal is..."**

If you completed the sentence with something like "A goal is something I need," you're a bit off track. If you completed the sentence with something like "A goal is something I <u>want</u>," congratulations. You have an excellent intuitive understanding of what goals really are.

Goals are wants

Goals are wants, not needs. They bridge the gap between where you are today and where you WANT to be tomorrow.

Goals are important because of the person they allow you to become in order to achieve them. A proper goal is an incentive to grow in awareness - awareness of your own inherent potential and goodness, awareness of the beauty and joy in the world around you, awareness of how you and the universe really work, and awareness of how you can use your knowledge and skills to create a better world for yourself and those around you.

That is a critical statement. <u>If you get caught up in running after goals just to check them off your list and forget the person you must become in the process, you may achieve some of your goals but you will do so with a gnawing emptiness inside of you.</u> Remember these key points:

- **You must become in order to achieve.**
- **What you become determines what you achieve.**
- **What you become is far more important than what you achieve.**
- **The real reason to set and achieve goals is to grow as a person.**

Why are goals important?

Every single aspect of your life, both your inner and outer worlds, is a direct reflection of your level of awareness. You cannot have, be, or enjoy anything until you become aware of it.

If you didn't know that there was a baseball game going on down the street, you couldn't enjoy the summer sun beating down on your tanned arms as you munched on a hot dog from your bleacher seat in center field.

Things do not just happen. **The universe works according to law.** If you weren't aware of your potential to earn $100,000 annually, you would never set a goal to even attempt to do it.

Stress-Free Success • 109

If you didn't know that you loved your spouse, why would you stay with him? If you weren't aware of the good things that he did for you, how could you compliment him for doing them?

If you had no idea that the universe works according to law, how could you ever live your life in accordance with the law? And, if you didn't know that Jesus died on the cross to forgive your sins, how could you be a Christian?

You get the idea. **It's impossible for you to do, enjoy, or be anything new until you become aware of it.**

More importantly, **it is possible for you to do, enjoy, or be <u>anything</u> new once you become aware of it.**

This is the real benefit of goal-setting.

When you choose a goal, your life immediately improves because you have become aware of a new direction for your life to take. As you progress toward achieving your goal, your life continues to improve because each step along the way increases your level of awareness.

This is why it is so critically important that you set and achieve goals that are meaningful to you. **Goals give you a reason and a method to continually raise your level of awareness.**

As your level of awareness increases, your life improves, naturally and almost effortlessly. Untold possibilities for creative expression and beautiful appreciation will unfold before you.

The true purpose of goals

As author, entrepreneur and speaker **Jim Rohn** says, "**The true purpose of goals is to compel you to become the person it takes to achieve them.**"

Prepare to be aware and let's move forward.

Lesson 9:
Use The 20 Laws Of Stress-Free "Goal-Getting"

The 20 Laws Of Stress-Free "Goal-Getting"
Goal achievement works the same way all the other processes in your life work - according to an unchanging set of fundamental laws and principles.

The first step in goal achievement is to understand these laws and principles so that you can put their incredible power to work for you.

Here are the laws for you to use:

• **Law #1: You must create or disintegrate. You cannot remain static.**

Nothing in the universe is static. Everything is in a constant state of change. Even as you read this sentence, cells in your body are dying and being replaced by new ones. You are constantly becoming a new person. Physicists will tell you that the electrons that form what we call physical mass are constantly whizzing through their orbits at great speed. They never rest.

Philosophers and religious leaders will tell you that Spirit (or God) is always for expansion. In each group's language, the words change, but the meaning is constant: Nothing remains the same. **Everything is either growing or dying, moving forward or moving backward, expanding or disintegrating.**

The same principle holds true for goal-achieving. When you set and pursue goals, you are actively creating a new, better life for yourself. If you choose not to set and pursue goals, you are giving up your chance to grow and expand. **If you are not growing, you are dying. There are no in-betweens, and there are no excuses.** You either move forward or you move backward. You cannot remain the same.

Stress-Free Success • 111

The choice is yours.

Why not choose growth?

- **Law #2: There is no try; there is only do.**

In *The Return of the Jedi*, Luke Skywalker crashed his ship in a remote area. His teacher, Yoda, tells him that he can raise it from the mud and muck with the power of his mind. Luke tries and tries and cannot seem to do it. He complains to Yoda who tells him, "There is no try. There is only do."

How true.

So many of us spend our entire lives "trying" without ever really accomplishing anything. **Saying "You'll try" is a copout.** It means you don't really believe you can do it (if you did it, you'd say, sure, I'll get that done) and it gives you an excuse when you don't get it done - "I tried."

Quit trying all the time and start doing.

The concept of **The Ultimate Scorecard** will help you keep this idea in your mind. I received this on e-mail one day, so I won't take credit for originating it, but I will say that it's one of the best "scorecards" I've ever seen:

The Ultimate Score Card

____ You either did or you didn't!
____ You are either winning or losing!
____ You are either moving closer or further from what you want!
____ You are either going for more or less!
____ You are either living or dying!
____ You either do it or don't!

Ask yourself...

"Is what I'm doing right now working for me or against me? Am I creating or disintegrating?"

Tell yourself...

DO IT NOW!

- **Law #3: The more important the source, the stronger the goal**

If you have ever taken a basic psychology class, you will remember Abraham Maslow and his famous Hierarchy of Needs. Maslow thought that there is a continuum that measures the importance, and hence the motivation, of various basic human needs.

The hierarchy started with basic survival needs such as food and water and moved to the top rung, which he called **self-actualization**.

Another way to look at the hierarchy would be to view the lower-level motivations as basically self-conscious. They are needs that are necessary to and satisfy only you. As you move up the ladder, your needs and actions affect an increasingly larger sphere. The self-actualization rung can then be viewed as your integration with the divine portion of your being.

To put this in terms of goal-achievement, your lowest level goals will be those that affect solely your physical nature. At a slightly higher level will be those that satisfy your intellectual nature. The highest level goals you will ever achieve are those that express your spiritual or divine nature.

The key to using this principle is to remember that **you cannot achieve goals on a level that is higher than your level of awareness.**

For example, if you do not realize that you do indeed have a spiritual nature, you won't be able to achieve goals that affect that part of your nature. This is why some people have tons of money and very little inner peace or satisfaction. Money exists on the physical level. They are living on the physical level. Inner peace and satisfaction come from the spiritual level. Until they increase their level of awareness, they will not be able to taste the fruits of this level of achievement.

Imagine yourself climbing a twisting road
up the side of a mountain. You get about 1000

> *feet up and look down over the valley below. You see all kinds of beautiful scenery that you could not see when you were living down below. A few hours later, you have reached a height of 5000 feet. Now, when you look down you see even more beauty and peace in the land around you. The land itself has not changed. The only thing that has changed is your level of awareness of its inherent substance and beauty.*

This is why it is so important to **remember the person that you're becoming** as you go through the process of achieving your goals. Raising your level of awareness will open your eyes to an entirely new landscape of life. This new landscape will hold all kinds of possibilities for achieving new and higher goals.

As you achieve new and higher goals, you will continue to become a more complete, more self-actualized person. And, as you grow as a person, the quality of your life will grow right along with you.

• Law #4: You will achieve your goal when you have a strong enough <u>reason</u> to achieve your goal

One of the places people get stuck when they go to achieve their goals is with reversing the order of reasons and answers. **Reasons come first, answers second.**

Until you have a reason for achieving a goal, you will not be motivated to take the action necessary to achieve it. When you have a strong enough reason, you will take the action almost without thinking of it.

> *Let's say your goal is to earn enough money to afford a new house. Your friend asks you why you want to do that. You tell her, "Oh, I just think it'd be nice to have a new house and I'm kinda ready for a change of scenery." If that's your reason, do you think you'd be very motivated to go out and do 37 cold calls a day to earn the money you need to buy the house? Now, let's say you put*

this principle to work and begin thinking about why you really want the new house.

The next time your friend asks you, you tell her, "I want a new $100,000 house with a two-car garage, three bedrooms on the second floor and a big yard out back because it is what my family and I deserve. My wife and I will be able to spend hours with our children playing in the yard, helping them do their homework in the study and watching movies together in the den. The kids will be proud to have their friends over to this beautiful home. My friends and co-workers will know how successful I am and how much I am providing for my family. The children will have a safe, happy place that will protect them from the influence of drugs, violence, and alcohol. My wife and I will be able to snuggle up together in front of the fireplace all winter and sit on the porch swing holding hands in the summer. That is why I want this new house."

Do you think that with a reason like that you might be just a little more motivated to go out and make cold calls and do all the other things that are necessary to achieve your goal?

I sure hope so.

When your reason is strong enough, you will find a way to achieve your goal. You will not find an answer without having a reason first, however.

When we begin the goal-setting process, keep this in mind. Focus on your reasons why and you will find a way to achieve your goals. As the saying goes, **"If the dream is big enough, the facts don't count."**

• Law #5: Fall in love with something you WANT.

The key term here is WANT. It is totally irrelevant what has happened in the past.

Don't let the past dictate the future or affect the present. When you are setting and achieving goals, you must **focus on enjoying the present while building for the future.**

You must **decide what you WANT, not what you need or think you can have.**

The universe works according to law. So does your life. You get just about what you expect.

Your thoughts determine the input into your subconscious; your subconscious goes to work to turn this input into reality; it triggers emotions which trigger actions which cause results.

Whatever you expect is what you will think about. This will be the image that forms in your subconscious which eventually will manifest in your life. Expect more, get more.

Expect less, get less.

It sounds simple, and it is, but it's true.

That's why poverty is a state of mind, not a state of the pocketbook. If you expect to be wealthy and imagine yourself as already wealthy in your mind, it will only be a matter of time before you become wealthy in the pocketbook.

As Mike Todd said, "I've never been poor, only broke. Being poor is a frame of mind. Being broke is only a temporary situation."

When you fall in love with something you WANT, you are harnessing all the power of the universe and putting it on your side in the race to turn your want into physical reality.

By deciding specifically what you want, you have chosen the thoughts that will enter your conscious mind. This will help create an image of you enjoying your want in your subconscious. The emotions you feel when you fall in love with this want are like kindling for your fire. Once lit, they will light all kinds of other resources and soon you will have a blazing inferno that is bursting forth to turn your dream into reality.

Here are the keys to <u>eliminating the three common roadblocks</u> along this path:

1. First, **quit focusing on what you need just to get by.** Think of this example: which gets you more excited about getting out of bed in the morning - earning $1,000,000 to pay off the mortgage on a new dream house and take your family on a trip around the world or working for a couple hundred bucks to just barely be able to pay the bills?

Unless you're real weird (and I doubt that you are) I'd guess that building a dream house is one heck of a lot more exciting than paying off a bunch of stupid bills.

2. Second, **quit limiting yourself by going after only those things you think you can have or that you deserve.** You have absolutely no idea how much potential is inside of you. Your prime responsibility as a creative expression of Infinite Spirit is to allow your inherent potential and goodness to unfold and bless your life and the lives of others around you.

<u>If you lower your sights to go after just what you think you can have or deserve, you are not fulfilling your responsibility as a human being.</u> You are selling yourself short. In the process, you are holding others back, because the ideas and things that you create could be just the spark they need to make more of their own lives.

3. Finally, **do not EVER let your present reality affect the goals you shoot for.** <u>Your present reality is only a reflection of your thinking and actions of the past. It does not, I repeat DOES NOT in any way reflect the potential inside of you or limit what you can do in the future.</u> That is entirely up to you.

Just because you thought or acted a certain way in the past does NOT mean you ever have to think or act that way again.

Stress-Free Success • *117*

You are in control.

You can choose to change the pattern anytime you would like.

Make that choice today. **Commit to making your life from this moment forward a beautiful masterpiece of human excellence.**

• **Law #6: All you have to know is WHAT you want. You don't have to know HOW to get it.**

Many people shortchange themselves by asking themselves HOW they are going to achieve their goal before they even set it.

They think, "Gee, I'd love to earn $1,000,000 this year."

Then they say, "How would I do that?"

They can't immediately come up with a workable plan so they give up the goal as "impossible."

No goal that you truly desire with all of your heart and which does not violate the natural laws of the universe is impossible.

Your responsibility is to decide WHAT you want. You then turn your WHAT over to your subconscious and let it do its job. It will go to work to create the circumstances and attract the resources that allow you to achieve your goal.

If, before you even started, you knew every step you had to take to achieve your goal, you could run right out and achieve it. You wouldn't have to stretch or grow much at all. That would be defeating the real purpose of setting and achieving goals.

The value of goals is that they cause you to expand your awareness, express more of your potential, and grow into a better person. In order to accomplish this, you need to set big goals that really cause you to stretch to reach them. They should be goals that get you totally fired up just thinking about them - goals that you can inject the power of emotion and desire into.

Trust the power of your own mind as well as the universe around you. Pick a big goal that really means something to you, one that you will have to really stretch to accomplish. Fix that goal in your mind, turn it over to your subconscious and trust the subconscious to do its work in attracting the circumstances and resources you need to turn your goal into reality.

To apply this idea, change the question that you ask yourself when you set a goal.

Instead of immediately saying, "How can I achieve this goal?", ask yourself, "What is the first step to achieving this goal?"

That's all you need to know. Take that step. When you have completed that step, you will see what the next step should be. When you have completed that step, you will see what the next step should be. And so on until you achieve your goal.

- **Law #7: The only reason you don't already have your goal is you're not aware of how to get it**

That may sound basic on the surface, but it is actually one of the most important concepts of goal-achieving. What it really means is that **everything you need to achieve your goal already exists.** The only thing you have to do is become aware of how to use it in a way that will achieve your goal.

> *Sand is one of the basic ingredients of silicon which is used to make silicon chips which power computers. Sand has been around for about as long as the earth itself has.*
>
> *Therefore, the raw materials that we needed to build computers that create billion-dollar fortunes and incredible advancements for society have always existed. It was not until the past 40 years, however, that anyone became aware of*

> how to use the raw materials in a way that would allow a computer to work.
>
> Ditto for flying. The laws of aerodynamics have always existed. It wasn't until the Wright Brothers set a goal to become the first men to fly, however, that we learned to use the laws of aerodynamics in our favor.

The same is true of your own goals. **All the resources and raw materials you need to achieve your goal already exist. You don't have to go out and create anything new. All you have to do is become aware of a better method for using what is already here.**

The power of this concept comes when you set lofty goals. Others may tell you they are "impossible." You may even think this yourself at times. The truth is, they are very possible, if you are willing to trust in your mind and dedicate yourself 100% to becoming aware of how to combine the resources at your disposal to turn your goal into physical reality.

> Think in terms of "Everything I need to accomplish this goal already exists. Each day I am becoming more aware of how to use these resources to accomplish my goal. I know that if I maintain my focus, I will achieve the level of awareness necessary to turn my goal into physical reality."

Notice that the key here is your level of awareness. All of us had the capability of using electricity, a force which has always existed, to power incandescent light bulbs. Thomas Edison was the first person to raise his level of awareness to the point where he could understand how to use this potential to create the electric light.

Focus on continually raising your level of awareness. The more you know about how your own mind and body works, as well as how the laws of the universe work, the easier it will be to combine the resources at your disposal in a way that will help you achieve your goal.

Just as importantly as achieving your goal, this increased level of awareness will mean that you are growing as a human being.

You are replacing your old, negative conditioning with new, more positive conditioning. You are fixing new positive images in your subconscious. These new images are triggering new sets of exhilarating, happy emotions. You find yourself naturally taking actions that improve your life. Daily, you are expressing more and more of your potential and inherent goodness. And you are realizing your true relationship with Infinite Spirit and the world around you. This is the true power of goals.

- **Law #8: You cannot give what you have not got.**
You can only give on the level you have.

Horace once said, "You cannot give what you haven't got." He was right. If a pastor does not have his own spirituality, he cannot give spiritual understanding to his congregation.

> If the Good Samaritan did not have money, he could not have helped the people in the village.
>
> If Ghandhi did not have love and compassion for others, he could not give his love and compassion away.
>
> If Martin Luther King did not have a dream, he could not have shared his dream.
>
> If Thomas Edison did not have wisdom and insight, he could not have given us the gift of his wisdom and insight.

Oftentimes, people say that one of their primary goals is to be able to help others and give things to them. That is a wonderful and meaningful goal and will surely help you grow into a better, more fully functioning human being.

If this is your goal, you must first get what you would like to give. If you want others to understand how to read, you must first understand the theory of teaching reading. Go learn it. If you want world hunger to diminish, you must first understand alternatives to providing food. Go find them. If you want us to live on a higher spiritual level, you must first live on this level yourself. Go enlighten yourself. If you want to teach others, you must first know what you are teaching. Go educate yourself.

This sounds very basic, but it is very important. **Many people eliminate any chance of ever achieving their goals because they run around trying to tell everyone else how to get something they have never got themselves.**

This hurts them in two ways. First, they can't do a very good job of helping or teaching someone, if they don't fully understand what they are doing. Second, they are compromising their integrity by not "walking their talk." They are saying one thing and doing another.

This violates the **law of cause and effect**. The changes that you want are effects of your ability to give your own insight and understanding. If you do not have them, you cannot give them, so don't expect to *get the effect that you want.*

• **Law #9: No more effort is required to pursue abundance than accept mediocrity.**

You are living in one of the most glorious, prosperous times ever in the history of the world. Technological innovations have allowed us to live in levels of comfort and luxury our ancestors couldn't even dream of. Even the poorest Welfare recipients in the U.S. are many times better off than much of the population in Third World and other poor countries.

It is your choice whether to actively demand your share of the incredible prosperity around you or passively settle for whatever mediocrity comes your way.

It takes no more effort to demand abundance than it does to accept misery.

After all, misery IS a full-time job. I mean, it's tough to be truly miserable without committing at least 3 hours a day to complaining and whining; 5 hours to watching TV; 1 hour to moping about how bad the world is treating you; and 2 more hours stuffing your face and engaging in other activities to try to take your mind off how miserable you've become. All <u>that adds up to 77 hours a week job, just to stay fully miserable.</u>

What would happen if you took all that time and energy and invested it solely in goal-achieving activities? Let's see... 77 hours a week of goal-achieving activities. I bet you'd see some awesome results, don't you?

And it wouldn't require any more time or effort than it does to be miserable.

Which one are you going to choose?

The choice is yours.

You already know that you must create or disintegrate. You cannot remain static. You are either pursuing abundance or accepting misery.

Which do you want to commit your life to? **Which ARE you presently committing your life to?**

- **Law #10: Kill your "pink elephants."**
   Concentrate on where you want to go and what you want to be, not where you don't want to go or what you don't want to be

Stress-Free Success • 123

Get out a pencil or highlighter right now and mark this phrase:

Your mind cannot function on the opposite of an idea.

When you say you don't want to do something, your mind misses the don't and goes to work to create exactly what you say you don't want.

The classic example is a pink elephant. Don't think of a pink elephant. What did you just think of? A pink elephant, of course.

The same concept works in all areas of your life.

If you say, "I don't want to get sick," what image are you focusing on? Sickness.

If you say, "I want to get out of debt," what image are you focusing on? Debt.

If you say, "I don't want him to hurt me anymore," what image are you focusing on? Pain.

If you say, "I don't want to be fat anymore," what image are your focusing on? Obesity.

In all of these cases, what is in control?

What you don't want and are afraid of getting is in control. And if it's in control, what do you think you're always going to get? Everything you don't want.

> As Vernon Howard once put it, "To be successful, there's nothing to do; there's only something to see."

That is what is beginning to happen to you now. You are beginning to see the light; you are getting an inkling of the keys to turning your life around; you are ready to break free from the ties that have bound you in the past.

How do you get rid of the last of the ties that hold you back?

Flip-flop your thinking. Focus on what you do want, not what you don't want. Think about where you want to go, not where you don't want to go or where you've already been.

Think, "I am healthy... I am wealthy and prosperous... I have positive, loving relationships... I have a lean, trim body." If you have trouble believing those phrases when you say them, modify them to say, "I am getting healthier every day... I am increasing my wealthy and prosperity daily... My relationships are becoming more loving all the time... My body is improving each day."

Either way, the result is the same. You are focusing your mind on what you do want in your life.

Your conscious thoughts are creating images in your subconscious mind. Your subconscious, being the dutiful servant that it is, goes to work immediately to turn these images into physical reality. It does not rephrase them or alter them in any way. It just accepts the exact orders it has been given (wouldn't it be great if your kids were like that?). Give it the proper orders. **Focus on what you want.** Create images of the good life you are moving toward. And trust in the power of your mind to make your good life a reality.

> *Doing this sets your mind on your goal like the homing system in a torpedo. As you move toward your target, you may get off course occasionally, but your inborn homing system will always correct your course and get you smoothly back on track to creating the image that you are focusing on.*

One more point before we move on to the next principle: Focus on what you are putting in, not what you are taking out. **Winners focus on how to put the most in.** Losers focus on how to get the most out.

- Winners say, "How can I add more value to my employer so that he willingly increases my salary?" Losers say, "How can I get him to pay me more money without working any more hours?"

- Winners say, "How can I treat my spouse better?" Losers say, "How can I get my spouse to do what I want?"
- Winner say, "How can I grow?" Loser say, "What is the minimum I can do to stay the same?"

Think like a winner.

· Law #11: Your barriers are imaginary; ignore them.

<u>Believing that we have to "break through" barriers is one of the biggest traps that most of us fall into</u> when we are thinking about making a quantum leap toward our goals. We hold ourselves back because we think that it's going to be too much work to "bust down the walls" that are preventing us from having our dreams. This whole notion is based on the common, but false, paradigm that these barriers even exist.

In reality, **there are no *true* barriers in our lives.**

<u>The only "barriers" that seem to stand between us and our goals are those that we put up ourselves by engaging in faulty thinking.</u>

There is always a way to achieve our goals, we're just not aware of it yet. Therefore, every single "wall" we reach is one we built through the delusions in our own mind. If we built the wall, we can surely take it down or walk right around it - instantly and permanently.

All it takes is a decision. Decide immediately that from now on you will live with the paradigm that all your barriers are imaginary, so you are perfectly free to ignore them.

Say it aloud, "Every single solitary barrier that I think is between me and my goal is purely a figment of my imagination. Since I created all these barriers in my imagination and that is the only place they exist, I am free to un-create them - now and forever. From this moment forward, I choose to ignore my barriers and pursue my dreams relentlessly and with joy in my heart."

Now repeat it three more times, saying it a bit louder each time, until it begins *to be ingrained in your mind.*

- **Law #12: You have no proof that you <u>can't</u> achieve your goals**

Most all of us have been guilty at one time or another of short-changing ourselves when it comes to achieving our goals. We are scared to reach for our B.U.D. (Big Ultimate Dream) because we aren't sure if we have what it takes to get it and we're not sure we want the responsibility that comes along with getting it.

> *After all, who are you to think that "little old me" can achieve all that? And, geez, even if I did achieve all that, I'd have no excuses and nothing to complain about and I might even have to let go of my mediocre friends, too.*
>
> *Gee willikers, that's an awful lot of change and responsibility just to achieve, oh, the biggest, most exciting dream I've ever had in my entire life, isn't it?*

Get rid of your pathetic little excuses and get going on pursuing your dream.

How much have you done in the past week to bring you closer to your Big Ultimate Dream?

That's right, not much.

That means you have almost no proof whatsoever that you cannot reach your goal. So you have no idea whether it's possible or not. All you can do at this point is speculate. Speculation is for losers. <u>The only way to know that you won't reach your goal is to never go after it.</u> Guaranteeing you'll never get what you really want is a pretty stupid way to live your life, don't you think?

Get out there and get busy proving to yourself that you can or cannot do it. Doubt your limits, not your abilities. Guess what? The more you get out there, the more you'll realize that it's not so hard after all. You've got all kinds of incredible talents just waiting to be expressed.

You can do it, so go do it.

- **Law #13: <u>What</u> you do is more important than <u>how</u> you do it**

>You could be the absolute best in the entire world at what you are now doing, but you would still never achieve your goals if you're not doing the right thing.
>
>If Babe Ruth had dedicated his life to becoming the best in the entire world at mowing the lawn, he would never have world a World Series ring or enjoyed the thrill of hitting a ninth-inning homer. In fact, we would probably have never heard of him.

Keep this in mind as you are setting and achieving goals.

What you do is more important than how you do it. **One of the major reasons we aren't succeeding nearly as much as we could be is because we're wasting our time doing the wrong things.**

We habitually do what we do best instead of finding the best things to do. If what you do best would allow you to achieve your goals, you would have already achieved them.

You may very well be at the top of the ladder, but is your ladder leaning against the wrong building?

Think about your profession.

What two or three things, if you did them consistently every day, would almost guarantee your success?

For me, those things are writing 2000 words and investing one hour in figuring out how to market what I write. For a real estate agent, those things might be making 25 calls to prospects and investing one hour in improving the listing presentation. For a CEO, the key things could be investing two hours in high-level strategic thinking and "walking the floor" to get the pulse of her company.

> For any of us, shuffling papers, hanging out at the coffee machine, running copies, opening mail, making routine bank deposits, and other such time-wasters are NOT the key things that will make a quantum difference in our level of success.

What you do is more important than how you do it.

I repeat that point because it is so important.

You can be rather average, but if you're doing the right thing, you will succeed anyway.

> You could be an average real estate agent who closes 25% of your listing presentations. One of your friends is a real pro at closing and nails 70% of the presentations she does. You call 32 prospects per day, or 160 per week. Your friend re-arranges files, sorts mail and other activities during the hour you invest calling on prospects. She averages 6 prospects per day. You both get about 10% of your prospects to allow you to do a presentation.
>
> At the end of the week, you've done 16 presentations and closed four of them. Your friend has done three presentations and closes two of them.
>
> At the end of the year, you will have earned about $250,000 more than your friend, despite the fact that you were an average agent whose closing ratio was less than half of your friend's.

What you do is more important than how you do it.

Get out a piece of paper now and write down the two or three things that will make the biggest impact on your success. Commit to doing them every day.

And add this to the end of your list: "No excuses. Period."

• Law #14: Think in terms of investment

Many people get bogged down in the goal-achievement process because they focus on what they think they are missing out on when they invest time or money in setting and achieving their goals. They take the viewpoint that "Gee, it's Saturday morning and I could be lying in bed, but no, I'm up early exercising, meditating, and reviewing my goals." Well, that's theoretically true, but let's put it in different terms. Let's begin to think of the hours you put into your goals as an investment.

> *Imagine you put in two hours per day or 14 hours per week working toward your goals. This is about 8 percent of your total hours in the week. Are you really saying that creating a better future is not worth investing 8 percent of your hours in? If that's true, put this book down and go back to bed now.*
>
> *You're a loser and you're gonna stay that way until you wake up and get a clue.*

The other common area where people mess up is thinking that money they spend on books, seminars, and other education is a cost. **A cost is money you spend for a one-time return. An investment is money you put to work to generate returns for many years to come. Education is one of the best investments you will ever make.**

Why?

Let's say you invest $1,000 in attending a weekend seminar. You get one good idea from this seminar and use that idea to earn an extra $50 a week. In five years, you will have earned $13,000 extra income on your $1,000 investment.

Compare that to the $469 you would have earned on a bond or CD that compounded at 8 percent annually.

Which is the best investment? There is no comparison.

Even if you had to attend five $1,000 seminars to get that one good idea, you would still generate many times more income than sticking the money in the bank or buying a government bond.

And, who can put a price on developing better self-awareness, more inner peace, more loving relationships with your family, and more happiness in your life?

What better investment could you ever make than one in yourself? **Think of the time and money you put into education and setting and achieving goals as the best investment you will ever make**, and you will be sure to stay on the right track to your goals.

• **Law #15: Your mind works according to law. Obey the law.**

Have you ever set a goal, tried to put together a plan that would get you to the goal, even started to execute the plan, and the wondered why it didn't seem like you were getting anywhere?

What probably happened was somewhere along the line you were attempting to disobey the laws of your mind. Your mind works according to definite laws and disobeying the laws never works.

Here are the five Laws of Mind:

1. Your mind cannot tell time. It does not understand the future tense. If your mind does not understand something, it will not go to work to create that something.

Write and think about your goals in the present tense. Think, "I am attracting $100,000 per month into my life," not "I will be earning $100,000 per month in five years." This puts your mind to work to turn your goals into reality. It keeps you from limiting your mind by putting artificial time limits on your goals (after all, you may be able to earn $100,000 per month in two years, if you let your mind go to work to figure out how). It also helps you enjoy the process of pursuing your goals as much as the momentary exultation of achieving your goals.

2. Your mind cannot invoke the opposite of something. Tell it, "I won't get a cold," and it will help you catch a cold because it glosses right over the "not" part of your statement. Instead think, "I feel great and I am getting healthier every day."

3. Your mind does not accept ultimatums. Have you ever told yourself, "I'll get thin or I won't go to the party next weekend," or "I'll get out of debt, even if it kills me to do it." While statements like that certainly place the power of emotion on your side, they do not work, because your mind is perfectly impartial. It does not accept ultimatums from you.

Saying "I will" do something violates our first rule - your mind cannot react to future tense. And statements like "even if it kills me to do it" are really stupid because what do you think your mind begins focusing on?

4. Your subconscious accepts anything put in it as real. This is why your thoughts are so critically important. You can run around all day saying aloud that you are successful and you will achieve your goal, but if you keep telling yourself that you're really a worthless little clod of ailments and you'll never reach your goal, that's what image will form in your subconscious. It will then act as the dutiful servant that it is, accept your statement at face value and go to work to turn it into physical reality.

Conversely, since your subconscious accepts anything you put into it as real, **you can pre-program your successes by thinking about them in the present**

tense. This is why present-tense visualizing is so effective. Each time you feel successful or think successful thoughts, you are creating success blueprints in your mind. Then, when you go to achieve a new, lofty goal, your mind sorts through all the images that it has and finds that you already have success blueprints that would indicate that you can indeed achieve that goal. Your goal achievement then matches the image that is already in your mind and the process becomes much easier and more natural.

5. Your mind gives you exactly what you dwell upon. Just as it accepts anything put into it as real, your mind will create in physical reality exactly what you dwell upon in your intellectual and emotional states.

Dwell upon success. You'll get success.

Dwell upon failure. You'll get failure.

Dwell upon nothing. You'll get nothing.

Dwell upon ambiguity. You'll get confusing ambiguity.

Be crystal-clear about exactly what you want, because whatever it is, that's exactly what you're going to get.

•Law #16: Success compounds

Success is just like your investment portfolio. It compounds over time. Unlike your investments, however, you can determine at what rate and how frequently it compounds. If you make small, steady gains in any area of your life, they will compound into huge returns in a very short time.

If you became just 1 percent better at something each day, over the course of a year, you would improve your ability to do it by almost 38 times.

Imagine that.

> *You could start improving your sales presentation by 1 percent today. If you were consistent with those small gains, you would be nearly 38 times more effective one year from today. What would that do to your income?*

Have you ever wanted to write a book but thought you would never be a good enough writer to get published? Start writing today. Improving by 1 percent each day will make you a 38 times better writer in one year.

Have you wanted to multiply your income? Figure out what you can do today to increase your income by 1 percent. If your average pay is $100 per day, figure out what to do to make an extra dollar today. Keep increasing your income by 1 percent each day, and you'll be earning $3,778 per day at the end of one year.

How's that for compound growth? And <u>all you had to do was steadily improve 1 percent each day and allow your gains to compound</u>.

This is a key principle to remember when you are setting your goals. **Never say a goal is impossible to achieve.** Even if you only earned $10 per day, you could increase your income by 1 percent daily and in two years, your daily earnings would compound to $14,270. If you run a network marketing organization, you could start with just yourself and increase your organization's size by just one half of one percent per day. In five years, you would have 8,975 people in your organization an would probably be earning a comfortable six-figure income, starting from zero today.

What if you aren't interested in earning money and would rather "change the world"? Follow the same principle.

> There are around 1 billion Christians worldwide. To go from one Christian to 1 BILLION, Christianity has grown at an average rate of just over 1 percent compounded for the 1995 years since Christ was born.
>
> That's it.
>
> Just about 1 percent growth each year.

If you grow your church or organization at 1 percent per week for 15 years, you will have 8,680 members for each 10 that you now have. And, if by speaking, writing, or some other means, your message reaches just 1 percent more people each day, you will have touched the lives of 77 million people in five years. What kind of sense of satisfaction would that give you?

<u>You can apply this principle to groups of people working together as well. It is especially powerful when applied to athletic or work teams.</u>

This is how Pat Riley coached his team to their NBA championship. Before the season began, he asked each player if he could improve by 1 percent in five key areas. If all 15 players improved by just 1 percent in those five areas, the team would be more than twice as good as it was the year before. This is how losers turn into winners in short periods of time and how you can turn any group you are associated with into a champion team in almost no time at all.

Now you can see why I call this **"The World's Most Powerful Success Principle."** Be consistent, be patient and compound your success. The results will amaze you.

• **Law #17: Five field goals beats two touchdowns every time**

You now understand how <u>small efforts, applied consistently, can compound into tremendous results.</u>

One of the best ways to be sure that you reach your goals is to use the concept of **targeting**. Targeting says that you will always aim for your target (your goal), but you will score points every time you get close. You can then feel a sense of achievement each time you score points. This allows you to celebrate growth and enjoy the process. An example from the world of sports will help illustrate.

The Dallas Cowboys are playing the Green Bay Packers. Each time the Cowboys get the ball, their goal obviously is to score a touchdown. They're having some trouble cracking the Green Bay defense, and in fact, they don't score a single touchdown the entire day. However, they do end up kicking five field goals. Green Bay obviously has the same goal- score a touchdown every time they have the football. They are more successful than Dallas because they put the ball in the endzone twice during the game. Unfortunately for them, Dallas' consistency in scoring little victories (field goals) five times, paid off. The Cowboys won the game 15-14.

Achieving your goals works the same way. **Consistent small victories will lead you to your ultimate victory.**

Want to sell $1,000,000 of your product this year? Twenty $50,000 sales will do it. Three $250,000 sales won't. That's not to say you shouldn't go after the big ones. Just make sure that you are setting up your game so that you can score consistently. As you learned in the previous section, **consistent small successes will compound into huge results.**

Don't forget, five field goals beats two touchdowns every time.

• **Law #18: Do the important things first and the urgent things later**

> Have you ever felt like there is always some "emergency" that comes up just when you are ready to get started on your goals? Join the crowd. Most people create "emergencies" on a regular basis and use them as a convenient excuse to never pursue their dreams.

Here's how to make sure you don't keep joining them:

Live your life <u>on purpose</u>. This means thinking of all your actions in terms of your mission and values.

Do the important things first and the urgent things later.

Read that sentence again because it is critically important. Do the important things first and the urgent things later.

Stress-Free Success • 136

The important things are those that lead your closer to your goals and dreams and those that are in harmony with your mission and values. Focusing on those things and you will find that most of the so-called urgent things get done by neglect. I know that may sound hard to believe, but it's true.

We are individual expressions of Infinite Spirit. Spirit is always for expansion. We express our spirituality and individuality through the creative pursuit of our dreams and goals.

This is growth.

To keep it straight in your mind, ask yourself, **"Will doing this seemingly urgent task really matter much in five years? Or will doing something to move me closer to my dreams and goals be more important?"**

If you are living on purpose, you will quickly realize that it means far more to live your dream than take out the trash or pull the weeds in the garden. Living your dream is expanding your being and growing into a fuller, richer, more complete person. It's pretty unlikely that you could say the same about taking out the trash.

If taking out the trash or pulling the weeds in the garden still seems ridiculously important to you, set a new goal for yourself: to earn enough extra income that you can pay someone to do these chores for you. Whatever you pay someone to do them will be worth it because you will free up all kinds of time and psychic energy that you can invest in pursuing your goals and living your dream.

You will never find time to set and achieve your goals. You must make time for them.

Do the important things first and leave the urgent things for later and you will have no trouble making time for achieving your goals.

- **Law #19: Forget about time management**

Forget about time management?

After all that's been drilled into your head about the importance of managing your time properly.

That sounds like heresy, I know, but it's critical to achieving your goals. **You see, it doesn't much matter how much time you spend doing something, what matters is whether you get it done.**

Replace your time management mentality with a results management mentality. **Manage results, not time.**

My goal was to write this book in three months or less. That was the result I wanted.

I could have kept the outdated time management paradigm and said, "OK, to get that done, I think I need to spend three hours a day writing." Then I would have sat down and written for three hours. I may or may not have written enough words to complete the book. Instead, I adopted the new results management paradigm.

I broke my goal down into manageable chunks and then managed those chunks. For me, I knew that if I wrote 2000 words per day, I would finish the book in 90 days. Writing 2000 words per day became my sub-goal, and it worked.

Not only did it give me a definite, measurable task to complete each day, it gave me an incentive to challenge myself. If I could improve my writing enough that I could finish the 2000 words in less time, I would free up hours that I could invest in other, pleasurable activities.

Originally, I figured it would take about three hours each morning to write the 2000 words. If I had set my goal as "Write for three hours," it probably would have taken me about three hours to complete the 2000 words.

As Parkinson's Law states, **"The amount of work will always expand to fill the time allotted to it."** *Instead, by managing results, and not time, I found that the extra momentum I built up when I got cranking* *on my writing allowed me to finish the 2000 words in less than two hours each morning.*

When setting your goals, remember to <u>manage results, not time</u>. Set goals that can be broken into measurable results. Then <u>commit to the results you want, NOT to spending a certain amount of time attempting to achieve the results</u>.

This is the biggest difference between true professionals and everyone else. Professionals commit to RESULTS. Everyone else only commits to ACTIVIITIES.

Results count. Activities don't.

Commit to results.

• **Law #20: You are already ready to start, so just do it. NOW.**

You can spend your entire life getting ready to be ready, and you'll never feel ready.

You already know that you have access to all of the power of the entire universe through the use of your subconscious mind. You probably also understand by now that all of the talent and potential you will ever have is already sitting inside of you. The only way you will ever know what abilities you have is by testing them.

How do you test them?

By doing something that moves you toward your goals. By taking the first step.

That's all it takes.

Put one foot in front of the other. Put your right foot out. Put your left foot out. Put your right foot out. Put your left foot out. Soon you'll be walking around the room.

Put your right foot out faster. Put your left foot out faster. Put your right foot out faster. Put your left foot out faster. Soon you'll be running down the hall.

Put your right foot out even faster. Put your left foot out even faster. Put your right foot out even faster. Put your left foot out even faster.

Soon you'll be winning every race you win. But you'll never win the race until you enter it.

Now, think about this for a moment. If you already have all the potential in the universe at your command and you already have an incredible reservoir of potential built up inside of you, what are you waiting for? **Step up to the starting gate. You are ready to win, so just do it. NOW.**

With that in mind, let's move on to learning what a goal is, why it is important to set goals, and how the goal achievement process really works.

Lesson 10:
Your Ideal Stress-Free Life

How goal achievement REALLY works

In the next section, we will add to your list of potential goals. The list you are creating could be called your Dream List. It should contain all the elements of the ideal life for YOU.

Think of this as the menu from which you will be selecting your goals. You are sitting in this cozy, little restaurant feeling warm and happy from the glow of the beautiful person sitting across the table from you and the sweet glass of wine you just finished.

It's now time to order your main course. You tell the waiter exactly what you want and how you want it cooked. He goes back to the kitchen and informs the chef of your choice. Your chef gathers all the ingredients necessary to prepare your meal. He begins combining them in exactly the right proportions and cooking them at exactly the right temperature to prepare the absolute best dinner you have ever tasted.

After you placed your order, you sit back to enjoy the ambience of the restaurant and a wonderful conversation with your dinner partner. You have no need and no desire to go into the kitchen and look over the chef's shoulder to supervise what he is doing.

You are absolutely unconcerned about what is going on in the kitchen because you know that this is the best chef in the city and he will prepare your meal exactly as you ordered it. You also know that the waiter will bring it to you piping-hot as soon as it is ready.

In what seems like almost no time at all, the waiter appears with a wonderfully arranged plate of the most delectable dinner you have ever seen. Your faith in the cook and the waiter is more than rewarded as you bite into the first bite of a succulent salmon fillet covered with a light honey sauce.

That is exactly how the goal-achieving process works.

The list you just created with all your dreams is your menu. You can choose any dish you would like from your Menu of Goal-Achievement. As you peruse the menu, you form images of each dish in your conscious mind. You use your conscious mind to choose your dish.

Then you describe EXACTLY what you want to your waiter, the link between your conscious and subconscious mind. You then sit back and relax, knowing that your perfect dinner will soon appear on your plate.

Your waiter dutifully repeats your exact instructions to the chef, your subconscious mind. The chef gathers all the ingredients necessary to create your perfect dish. In the case of goals, your subconscious chef has the unique ability to go anywhere in the kitchen of the universe to gather all the ingredients for the achieving of your goal.

Once the chef has all the ingredients, he begins to mix them and cook them in the exact proper proportions. The aroma wafting from the kitchen tells you that he is cooking them, just like you will be able to "smell" it when your goal is getting near.

A few minutes later, the waiter reappears carrying your perfect dish, the same way your goal will appear in your life.

Just like in ordering a meal in a restaurant, there are a couple of **key things to remember** to make sure that you get exactly what you want:

- You decide what you want by forming images of all the possibilities in your mind and picking the dish with the most attractive image.

- You must tell your waiter <u>exactly</u> what you want. You don't just say, "Oh, give me anything," and expect him to bring you exactly what you want. In the same way, if you don't have a VERY specific goal, don't expect it to ever show up in your life.

- Don't bother the cook. Can you imagine going into the kitchen of Spago or one of the country's other great restaurants and leaning over Wolfgang Puck's shoulder to make sure he is doing everything properly? Not trusting the ability of your subconscious to gather the ingredients and mix them all into the right combination for your goal to turn into reality is like not trusting the ability of the cook to prepare your meal properly.

    It's like leaning over the cook's shoulder and constantly trying to put in different ingredients in your meal. You have no clue what the recipe for the meal is, so there's no way you could know if what you were suggesting was right or not. Each time you grabbed something out of the pot and pulled it up to see how it was cooking, you would be screwing up the cook's careful preparation.

Each time you try to change your goal, you're screwing up your subconscious' preparation to make your dream come true. It has to scramble around and gather a new set of ingredients, start mixing them differently, and basically just start over. Obviously, if you keep having your chef start over, it's gonna be a long while before you ever get the meal you want.

This is why focus is so important. If you stay 100% focused on your goal, it WILL turn into reality. Of that you can be sure.

Most of us have trouble staying 100% focused because we're not exactly sure what we really want.

Our waiter comes out and we order a filet mignon. He relays the order to the chef, who starts to prepare it. Then we change our mind. We call our waiter over and tell him we'd rather have chicken dijon. He rushes back to the kitchen and tells the chef, who has to throw out our half-cooked filet and start over again. We resume talking to our dinner partner.

Then a new idea suddenly hits us. We think maybe some veal oscar would be a perfect main course. Our waiter rushes back into the kitchen and tells the chef we changed our mind again. Out goes the half-baked chicken, in goes the veal oscar.

This process goes on and on and on.

It's no wonder that we rarely reach our goals. Now, you can be one of the few who easily and naturally turn your dreams into reality by staying focused on the goals you really want to achieve.

At this point, you have a solid understanding of who you are and how you fit into the world around you; you have learned how to use your mind to create any circumstances you would like in your life; and you have re-awakened your ability to dream and come up with a "menu" of potential goals and accomplishments that you would like to attract into your life.

Now, it's time to choose goals that lead you toward your ideal life. Let's get started...

How to decide what you *really* want out of life

Quick. Tell me exactly what you want out of life.

If you are like most people, you would have trouble answering that question when put on the spot like that. Most of us would say something like "To have a family."

Well, indefinite one, you could "achieve" your goal of having a family by getting a family of rodents that took up residence in your house.

But that's not what I meant, you say.

Well, that's what you said.

> *The universe and your subconscious mind are quite literal. They take what you tell them at face value. In order to set meaningful goals, you must know exactly what you want and why you want it and you must communicate*

this information accurately to your subconscious so that it can help you get it.

Here is how to figure out exactly what you want and what goals you should set:

The 3-Step Process For Defining Your Ideal Life
1. *Find out where you are now*
2. *Find out where you want to be*
3. *Decide why you want to be there*

In order to answer these questions thoroughly, we are going to re-visit some of the thought processes that you used earlier in the book to create your Dream Book.

Step 1: Where are you now?

You can't develop a sound plan for going forward to where you want to be until you know where you are starting from. If you wanted to get to Kansas City, but you didn't know where you were, you'd have trouble figuring out where to go, wouldn't you? If you were in Los Angeles, it would be easy to figure out that you would head east. If you were in New York, it'd be easy to figure out you'd head west. If you didn't know where you were, you'd have no idea whether to head east, west, north, or south.

Give yourself a Personal Success Check-Up. Answer the following questions in writing now.

- *What are you good at?*
- *What do you like to do?*
- *What do you currently do the most of?*
  List the activities you spend at least five hours per week on.
- *What three things that you have accomplished are you the most proud of?*
- *Name three things you've done that you are not proud of*
- *What are the most important things you've ever learned?*
- *How well are you living up to your mission in life?*
- *On a scale of 1 to 10, how would you rate*
  - *Your personal level of development and understanding*
  - *Your relationships with family and friends*

- Your level of career success
- Your financial standing
- Your emotional health
- Your physical health
- Your social life
* What is your current annual income?
  * How much of this income is passive-residual income?
  * How many hours do you work to earn this income?
  * Divide your income by your hours. What are your earnings per hour?
* What is your current net worth?
  * What are the sources of this worth- businesses, stocks, other?

Answering those questions gives you a very accurate answer to the question, "Where am I now?"

When you are done, go back and compare your answers to the ones you wrote down in the earlier section where you rated your life in the various areas. Has anything changed?

Now, let's move to step two, deciding exactly where you want to be...

Step 2: Where do YOU want to be?

Where DO you want to go?

For most of us, that's a hard question.

> We can usually tell you exactly where we don't want to go, but it's often much more difficult to describe exactly where we do want to go. That's because we spend most of our time thinking of all the things we don't want in our lives and all the things we want to avoid instead of focusing on our dreams and goals and exactly what we do want our lives to be like.

The result of this faulty thinking is that when we do sit down and try to put together some kind of plan of action to make our lives better, it is virtually impossible for us to do.

> It's like the story in Alice in Wonderland where Alice comes to the junction in the road that leads in different directions. She asks the Cheshire Cat for advice.
>
> > "Cheshire Puss... would you tell me please, which way I ought to go from here?"
> >
> > "That depends a good deal on where you want to get to," the Cat said.
> >
> > "I don't much care where..." Alice said.
> >
> > "Then it doesn't matter which way you go," the Cat said.

Don't be like Alice.

Begin right now to define exactly where you want to go.

Dream-building

To begin deciding where you want to go, we'll use the process of Dream-Building. Basically, Dream-Building means to let go of the past and soar high into a future where you can have anything you want and be anyone you want to be.

Let your imagination fly. Dream like a child.

> "Dream lofty dreams, and as you dream, so you shall become. Your vision is the promise of what you shall one day BE; your IDEAL is the prophecy of what you shall at last unveil. The greatest achievement was at first, and for a time, a dream. The oak sleeps in the acorn; the bird waits in the egg; and in the highest vision of the soul, a waking angel stirs. Dreams are the seedlings of realities. Your circumstances may be uncongenial, but they shall not long remain so, if you but perceive an ideal and strive to reach it. You cannot travel within, and stand still without." **James Allen**

> "There is nothing like dream to create the future. Utopia today, flesh and blood tomorrow." **Victor Hugo**

> "The future belongs to those who believe in the beauty of their dreams." **Eleanor Roosevelt**

Make the future yours by starting to believe in the beauty of your dreams today.

Your Life's Questions

Most of us are not used to dream-building. We have been beaten down for years and told we can't do that or there's no way we'll ever have that. You already know that those are lies. **You can do whatever you decide you want to do. And you can have whatever you decide you want to have.**

Continue the process that we started when you began producing your Dream Book earlier by answering these questions, in writing.

- What would I go for if I knew I could not fail?
- If I could be anyone I wanted to be, who would it be?
- If I could accomplish any 3 things, what would they be?
- If I could succeed in any career I chose, what career would I choose?
- If I could travel anywhere I wanted, where would I travel?
- If I could live anywhere in the world, where would it be?
- If I could live in any house I wanted, what would it look like?
- If I could drive any car I wanted, what would I drive?
- If I could dress any way I wanted, what would I wear?
- If I could have any 5 material things, what would they be?
- If I could have the perfect family life, what would it be like?
- If I could have the perfect spouse, what would he/she be like?
- If I could select my perfect friends, who would they be or what would they be like?
- If I could have the best social life, what would I be doing?

- *If I could look any way I wanted, how would I look?*
- *If I could become an expert at anything, what would I become an expert at?*
- *If I could have the perfect spiritual relationship, what would it be like?*
- *If I could meet anyone I wanted, who would I want to meet?*
- *If I could earn as much money as I wanted, how much would I earn?*
- *If I could experience anything I wanted, what things would I experience?*
- *If I could learn anything I wanted, what would I want to learn?*
- *If I could found or contribute to three causes, what would they be?*
- *If I could solve any one problem, what would it be?*
- *If someone gave me $10,000,000 today, what would I do with it?*
- *If I could have any three wishes, what would I wish for? (You can't wish for more wishes)*
- *What are the 3 craziest, most off-the-wall things I would like to do or have? (Don't worry about what your neighbors think- they don't.)*

Now get out a few more clean sheets of paper and think about your answers to those questions while you describe your perfect life.

- **What would my perfect day, week, or month be like?** Where would I be? Who would I be with? What would I be doing?

- **In 5 years, what would I like to be doing?** What kind of person would I like to have become? Where will I be living? Who will I be spending time with? How much will I be earning? What knowledge will I have acquired? What kinds of experiences will I have had? What will my typical day be like?

- **In 10 years, what would I like to be doing?** What kind of person would I like to have become? Where will I be living? Who will I be spending time with? How much will I be earning? What knowledge will I have acquired? What kinds of experiences will I have had? What will my typical day be like?

- **In 20 years, what would I like to be doing?** What kind of person would I like to have become? Where will I be living? Who will I be spending time with? How much will I be earning? What knowledge will I have acquired? What kinds of experiences will I have had? What will my typical day be like?

- **If I could live my perfect life, what would be my highest desires or goals in each area of life?** In other words, what 3-5 things would I like to accomplish more than any other in each area:
  Financial
  Career and professional
  Educational and personal development
  Social (including hobbies)
  Spiritual
  Relationships
  Health and fitness (including sports)
  Material (houses, cars, boats, planes, clothes, etc)

- Now look at the list you've just created and ask, **"What else is POSSIBLE?"** Add any totally wild things you've ever thought would be neat to do. Have you ever wanted to score a touchdown in the Super Bowl or race in the Indianapolis 500 or skate in the Olympics? Add them to the list.

- **Next add your biggest dreams that at this point you may not even think are possible.** Have you ever wanted to make $1 billion in a year? Be elected president? Walk on the moon? Put anything you think would be neat to do on your list.

Reach for your B.U.D., your Big Ultimate Dream

You've been working hard. Now you are ready to reach for your B.U.D., your Big Ultimate Dream.

> Think of your B.U.D. as the meal you are selecting from your Menu of Ideal Life. Since this is a mighty fine restaurant you are eating in this evening, your appetizer, salad, vegetables, bread, drink, and dessert all come with your meal. All you have to do is tell your waiter what appetizer you want, what dressing on your salad, what you would like to drink, and what you want for dessert. He will put the order in to your chef and you can rest assured that when your meal arrives, it will include everything you want.

Think of your B.U.D. the same way. It is your main course. When you select your main course, you will automatically get your appetizer, salad, vegetables, bread, drink and dessert. When you achieve your B.U.D., you will automatically achieve many of your other goals in the process.

Staying focused on one Big Ultimate Dream allows you to gather all of the resources available to you to achieve that dream and then get them all going in the same direction so your dream turns into physical reality in the shortest amount of time possible. Think of a cowboy out on the range. If his herd is running in every which direction, he will wear himself out trying to get them where he wants to go. If, on the other hand, he hitches his horses together, he can sit back in his wagon and enjoy the ride as he benefits from the power of all the horses pulling together in the same direction.

Another way to think of the benefits of focusing on your Big Ultimate Dream is to visualize light. A 100 watt bulb in your kitchen gives you a nice soft interior light. The same light particles however, can be gathered and focused so that they are all going in the same direction. When this happens, we get a laser that can cut diamonds. Same particles, more focus, equals many times more power. Your B.U.D. is your laser beam. It cuts through all the extraneous crap and gets to exactly where you want to go. Along the way, it will reveal to you ways to accomplish your other important dreams as well.

For example, let's say you want to build a new $250,000 house, take a trip around the world, write a best-selling novel, and spend more time with your family. What B.U.D. would be best to choose?

That's an individual decision that you have to make for yourself. There is no right or wrong B.U.D. and no right and wrong goals or dreams. You must choose something that really gets you excited.

In this case, one way to laser-beam focus your resources would be to choose "I have earned $1,000,000 this year while living a healthy, balanced life." When you achieve this B.U.D., you will naturally be able to build your house, travel around the world, cut back on your current job so you have time to concentrate on writing your novel and spend more time with your family. **Achieving your B.U.D. naturally and effortlessly allowed you to achieve many of your other goals.**

Which B.U.D. are you gonna reach for?

Get out a piece of paper and think about your B.U.D. Look back over your list of dreams that you completed in the section before. Spend a few minutes thinking about them. Answer these questions:

- **Prioritize your list of dreams**. Divide your list into A, B, and C dreams, according to their level of importance. A dreams are those that you feel like you have to accomplish to have reached your level and to have lived a happy, satisfying life. Include 5-10 dreams on your A list. Then group the rest of your dreams into the B list of dreams you would love to accomplish and the C list of dreams that it would be nice to accomplish but that you don't get all that fired up about at this point.

Now revise your A list based on your answers to these questions:

- **Accomplishing which 5 dreams would mean the most to you?**
- **Which 5 dreams on your list could you get the most emotionally involved in?** (In other words, which ones "light your fire", either because you believe in them passionately or because you would be totally excited to achieve them.)
- **In the next five years, pursuing my heart's desire in which area of life (financial, career, relationships, emotional, spiritual, health, or another) would give me the most satisfaction and contribute the most to my overall mission in life?**
- **What would you trade your life for?** (Not what would you die for - this means what is important enough that you would trade your waking hours to accomplish it and then feel like the trade was a good one.)

Add your answers to these questions to your A list and take off any dreams that now seem less important and place them on your B list. Now get ready to reach for your B.U.D.

Before you do, though, study the following section about goals not to choose.

The "Success System" that never works

Now you have a list of possible goals. The next thing we will look at is what things to immediately eliminate from your list, or what goals you should never choose. Here are the rules to follow:

- **Never set a goal to eliminate what you now have.**

How many times have you tried to "get rid of a bad habit" or "quit smoking" or "lose your extra weight" or "get out of debt"?

How many times have you succeeded at doing it?

Probably never.

Stress-Free Success • 153

Why?

By setting a goal to eliminate what you already have, you're focusing your thoughts on the very thing you want to get rid of.

Remember, your mind can't focus on the opposite of an idea. All it hears is "bad habit, smoking, extra weight, or debt". It then goes to work to maintain the thing you're trying to get rid of.

> To illustrate this idea, imagine that you are out exploring and you decide that you want to see five more miles of the river you are navigating today. You have two choices. You can swim upstream or you can float downstream. If you swim upstream, you may make progress for a little while, but you sure are going to get tired in the process. It's a whole lot easier and more productive to just relax and allow yourself to float gently downstream.
>
> Setting goals works the same way. If you set a goal to eliminate what you already have, you are swimming upstream.
>
> In effect, you are trying to violate the natural laws of the universe because your body and mind are not made to work that way. Make it easy on yourself by floating downstream. Follow the natural laws of the universe by setting your goals for what you would like to attract into your life, not what you want to get rid of.

Why does it work better this way?

Nature hates a vacuum. **When you eliminate one thing, the space doesn't just sit there empty. It's filled with something. One thing is always replaced with another. If you eliminate a bad habit, it is replaced with something. If you don't replace it with a good habit, it will be replaced with another bad habit.**

If you eliminate one kind of debt, it will be replaced with another kind of debt - unless you replace the "space" with financial abundance.

If you quit smoking, you will have the urge to begin again - until you replace the old habit with a new, healthier one such as exercising or reading.

If you lose weight, you will gain it all back - until you replace your old habits with new habits that keep it off.

- **Happiness and peace of mind are not goals.**

Many people make the mistake of setting goals "to be happy" or to "have peace of mind." <u>Happiness and peace of mind are not goals. They are conditions of life.</u> They come as a result of the higher degree of awareness that you achieve by doing the things necessary to reach your goals.

For example, let's say your goal is to become a millionaire in five years. Since money is a reward for service rendered, the only way you can do this without violating natural laws is to provide enough service that others will reward you with at least $1,000,000 in the next five years.

How would you provide this service?

There are hundreds of different businesses you could run, products you could sell, or services you could offer. The important thing to remember is, no matter which you choose, you'll be focusing much of your time on providing a benefit to other people, whether that is employees, customers, clients, suppliers, readers, seminar attendees, or whatever form it takes for your particular business.

Would you agree that if you are focusing on providing service to others, you will be growing as a person?

Would you also agree that as you grow, you'll become aware of more opportunities to be happy or to enjoy peace?

This is the proper order of this cause and effect relationship. **Your goals cause you to grow. Your growth causes you to live on a higher level of awareness. The effect of this whole process is increased happiness and peace of mind.**

- **Enlightenment is not a goal.**

Enlightenment is a state of being, just like happiness or peace. It is not a goal.

> *There is no way to measure enlightenment or to say, "Yessiree, I am now enlightened. I've achieved my goal."*

Enlightenment can only be experienced by living fully in the present moment. It comes from an understanding of how things really are, beyond the veils of our perception and conditioning.

If we try to set enlightenment as a goal, we are saying that it is something "out there" that we have to do something to get. If we are running around searching for a way to "achieve" enlightenment, we are focusing on the "out there" instead of the "in here." This assures us that we will never experience enlightenment because we are not fully here in the present moment.

Enlightenment comes from "in here," deep down inside of ourselves. It is a unique state of being in which you experience the world without your limited physical eyesight and conscious mind clouding your vision. It comes from fully integrating the spiritual nature of your being into your everyday existence.

Keep this in mind when you're setting and achieving goals. Be here now. That's how you come closer to experiencing enlightenment.

Choose Your Big Ultimate Dream

Now, you are ready to choose your Big Ultimate Dream. Answer these questions:

- **What single Big Ultimate Dream are you passionate about achieving?**
  - Look at your A list of dreams. What single Big Ultimate Dream will help you achieve the largest number or most important of your A list dreams?
  - **Write your B.U.D. here:**

  _____

  - **Write "My Perfect Life" or "My Big Ultimate Dream" across the top of a sheet of blank paper. Write your B.U.D. in BIG, BOLD letters below it.**

  That is your main course. Now let's learn how to decide if this is really what we want to order and then how to order our main course so that we will be assured of getting exactly what we want.

Defining Your Ideal Stress-Free Life, Step 3: Determine WHY you want to be there

As you've already learned, in order to achieve your goals in the most efficient manner possible, you must become emotionally involved with them. Reasons come first, answers second. **When the why gets strong, the how gets easy.**

Picture yourself having achieved your B.U.D.

- Can you clearly see yourself on the screen of your mind in possession of your B.U.D.?

- Do you seriously want to achieve your B.U.D.?

- Is this the most desirable, most exciting dream you can think of to achieve?

If you answered no to any of those questions, you need to re-think your B.U.D. You've probably done of three things:

- Chosen a B.U.D. that you think you should choose, because of what society, your family, or your friends have told you or made you think instead of a B.U.D. that you really want to choose, because of what you really feel and believe deep down inside you

- Chosen a B.U.D. that is too small and doesn't really get you excited or cause you to grow to achieve it
- Chosen a B.U.D. that is too large for your present belief levels. If you absolutely cannot see yourself achieving your goal, lower it slightly until you can see yourself achieving it. If you can't imagine earning $1,000,000 per day, lower your B.U.D. to $1,000,000 per year, or $1,000,000 in the next ten years.

> Be careful about lowering your B.U.D. too far, though. Remember, this is your Big ULTIMATE Dream. Once you have chosen it, you will be 100% focused on it and will NOT be changing it. You have incredible reservoirs of talent inside of you that have never been tapped, so before you lower your B.U.D., remember that as Napoleon Hill said in Think and Grow Rich, **"Anything you can conceive and believe, you can achieve."**

You have already conceived of it.

All that is left is for you to believe it.

It is often better to work on eliminating your limiting beliefs and change your paradigms about what is possible than it is to lower your B.U.D. to a level that won't really push you to become all that you can be. That is why we studied your beliefs and values at the beginning of this book. You now have a good understanding of how to choose a different set of beliefs, program it into your subconscious mind, and continue forming the image of you with that belief until it becomes a part of your new conditioning.

Following this process, you can alter your belief systems so that you begin to really believe you CAN achieve your super-B.U.D. By following the steps you've learned in this book, once you believe it, you not only CAN achieve it, you WILL.

How is irrelevant at this point

Since you will be tapping into the power of your subconscious mind and your subconscious mind is by its very nature infinite, you have no idea at this point what is or isn't possible. Nor do you have any idea of all the resources available to you or all the ways they could be combined to help you achieve your B.U.D.

Therefore, **it is unreasonable to think that you should now know exactly HOW you are going to achieve your B.U.D.** You may have a general idea, and you may know the first step you will take, which is wonderful, but you cannot predict in advance every single thing that must occur before you achieve your dream.

If you think you do already know exactly how to achieve your dream, go back to the prior section and choose a bigger dream. The whole purpose of your dreams and goals is to cause you to stretch and to grow. If you know all the things you need to do, you are not stretching and growing and you need a bigger B.U.D.

The Acid Test for B.U.D.'s

You have conceived your Big Ultimate Dream and clearly defined it. You can picture yourself living your dream. You believe that you can have it, although you don't know exactly how you will get it. Now it is time to give your B.U.D. the Acid Test to determine whether this is the right B.U.D. for you. The Acid Test consists of three parts:
- **The Reason Why**
- **The Growth Factor**
- **The Value Match**

The Reason Why

Go back to your sheet of paper where you wrote down the description of your B.U.D. Below your description of your B.U.D., write, **"Why I want and deserve to live my dream"** Then answer that question. Write down in as much detail as you can, EXACTLY why you want and deserve to achieve your B.U.D.

- *What pleasure will you get from achieving it?*
- *What pain will you experience if you don't achieve it?*
- *What other goals will achieving this B.U.D. naturally cause you to accomplish?*
- *What else will achieving this B.U.D. allow you to do?*
- *What makes you the happiest and most excited about achieving this B.U.D.?*

If you cannot articulate a good reason why you want to achieve your B.U.D., your B.U.D. has failed the Acid Test.

Purpose is stronger than object. You can set a goal to build a $1,000,000 house, but you will never take the actions necessary to earn the income to allow you to build it until you have a strong enough reason why you want to live in a $1,000,000 house. **If you don't have a reason why, you don't have a proper B.U.D.**

The Growth Factor

"The deepest personal defeat suffered by human beings is constituted by the difference between what one was capable of becoming and what one has in fact become." **Ashley Montagu**

"Of all the words of women and men, the saddest are these- I might have been." **Jeff Smith**

Now that you have defined the reasons why you want to achieve your B.U.D., write down your answer to these questions:

- **What kind of person must I become to achieve this goal?**

Once you've described the type of person you must become, you can complete the Growth Factor section of the Acid Test by answering these questions:

- *Is this the type of person I would like to become?*
- *Is this type of person in harmony with my values and my mission?*

If you answered yes to both questions, your B.U.D. has passed the second part of the Acid Test.

The Value Match
Many people achieve their goals but still suffer from a profound sense of emptiness inside because they achieved goals that conflicted with their values.

The sense of emptiness is their body's way of telling them that something is not congruent in their life. They do not have laser-beam focus on their perfect life, because part of them is moving toward goals that do not match their values. If you put your exterior affairs in the proper perspective by aligning them with your inner awareness, you will enjoy your success as well as achieve it. You will achieve your goals AND have a wonderful sense of inner peace and happiness by making sure that the goals you set are in congruence with your values, BEFORE you begin moving toward achieving your goals.

That Value Match is the second part of the Acid Test. Here are the questions to ask to be sure your B.U.D. passes the Value Match:

- *Is the reason you want material things a valid reason?* If you wrote down that you wanted a new house to make you happy, you'll never be happy because exterior things like houses are not the source of your happiness. The house could give you an outlet for creative expression or be a warm, cozy place to share love with your family, but it in and of itself will not cause you to be happy. Neither will any other material possession.
- *Does your B.U.D. and your reasons for achieving it match your values?* Look at your list of values. When

you achieve your B.U.D. will you be able to live your value?

- *Does your B.U.D. help you to move closer to your ultimate mission or purpose in life?* Making a lot of money is not necessary if your mission is to achieve oneness with God or Spirit. If, on the other hand, your mission is to help others, making money may be a wonderful B.U.D. Even though you will not need the money yourself, you can use it to do all kinds of good for others.

- *Are your B.U.D. and the other goals you will achieve along the way in line with each other?* Having sex with a new woman every week and having a loving relationship with your wife are probably not compatible goals. Partying every night and becoming an Olympic gold medalist are probably not compatible, either. When you find goals that are out of harmony like this, it probably means that you are not clear about what your values really are. Go back to the section on determining your values, beliefs, and life purpose and study it again.

If you answered yes to all four questions, your B.U.D. passed the Acid Test.

Congratulations.

A FREE GIFT FOR YOU before we move on: *To help you move smoothly through this step toward Stress-Free Success, I've prepared a* **Special Report titled, "Stress-Free Success: Phase Two."** *This Special Report gives you the advanced strategies you need to benefit from these ideas even more quickly and effortlessly. Normally, this Special Report is $10, but as a reader of this book, I'm offering it to you* **FREE**, *as my gift to you. I do ask, however, that you cover the $3 for shipping and handling to get your report to you. A form for requesting your FREE Report is at the back of this book.*

Lesson 11:
Turn Your Dream Into An Achievable Goal

The 4-Step Process for Achieving Your Goals
In order to turn your dream into physical reality, you will follow four steps:

1. Turn your dream into a goal
2. Harness your unseen resources and make them work for you
3. Close the GAAP: Complete your action plan
4. Execute your plan and enjoy the process

Step 1. Turn your dream into a goal
In the prior section, you analyzed your beliefs and values and chose a Big Ultimate Dream that was in harmony with those beliefs and values. At this point, you don't know exactly how you will achieve that dream and you haven't determined what resources you will need. The dream you chose is just that - a dream. Now it is time to turn your dream into a true goal.

Get out the sheet of paper that you wrote your B.U.D. down on and review it once again.

- *Does it still "feel right" to you?*
- *Are you still excited about achieving it?*
- *It is a big enough and important enough dream that you are willing to invest whatever it takes for as long as it takes to achieve it?*

Affirmative answers to those questions mean you are on the right track. Your big ultimate dream will serve as a wonderful primary overall goal.

How to phrase your Primary Overall Goal (POG)
Get out a new sheet of paper and write "My Primary Overall Goal (POG)" at the top of the sheet. Rewrite your B.U.D. by keeping these points in mind:

1. Write in present tense.

Phrase it as "I have..." "I now..." or "I am..." and then your goal. Some examples: "I have earned $1,000,000," "I have built my dream house on the water," "I am spending two hours a night with my family," "I now make $100,000 per year." Using present tense "tricks" your subconscious mind into helping you achieve your goal more quickly.

When your subconscious gets the message that you have already done something, it goes searching through its files to figure out when you did it. Of course, it comes up empty-handed since you haven't done it yet. Being the ever obedient servant that it is, it then decides, "Oh, gee, if she thinks she's already done this thing and I can't find any record of having achieved it, I must have missed one of my orders somewhere along the line. I'd better go to work immediately and create that record so I don't get in trouble for not obeying orders." Your subconscious then puts the gears in motion that will help you turn your dream into reality.

If you make the common mistake of phrasing your goal in the future tense ("I will make $1,000,000"), your goal does not serve as a catalyst to get the gears spinning. Your subconscious thinks, "Oh, she will make $1,000,000. I know she hasn't done it yet, but if she will do it sometime in the future, then I can sit back and take it easy for a while before I start helping her get it done."

Another benefit of phrasing your goal in the present tense is that you can begin to enjoy the benefits of achieving your goal today. You know that you exist simultaneously on three planes: the conscious, the subconscious, and the physical.

Believe it or not, you already have achieved your goal on two of the three levels. When you chose your goal, you possessed it on the intellectual, conscious level. When you envisioned yourself having achieved that goal, you were creating an image in your subconscious. This means you already possessed your goal on this level as well. The only thing left for you to do is achieve your goal on the third level, the physical.

While you are taking action to achieve your goal on the physical level, you can continue to enjoy already having achieved your goal on the spiritual and intellectual level.

Let's say your goal is to earn $1,000,000. Through your thought and imagination, you have already earned $1,000,000 on the conscious and subconscious levels. You can act as if you already are a millionaire, talk like a millionaire, think like a millionaire, view the world in the way a millionaire would view the world, react to opportunities and crises as a millionaire would react to opportunities and crises, behave like a millionaire would behave, and treat others as a millionaire would treat others.

You can also share the benefits of your goal with others through words and feelings. Words are an expression of you claiming your goal on the conscious, intellectual level. Feelings are an expression of you having claimed your goal on the subconscious, spiritual level.

By claiming your goal in the present on the conscious (intellectual) and subconscious (spiritual) levels, you are free to do all these things. And most importantly, by doing all these things - by acting and thinking as if you have already achieved your goal on all three levels, instead of just two - you will shorten the time until you can enjoy your goal on the physical level as well.

This brings us to the next important point for phrasing your POG:

2. Give your Primary Overall Goal a date for achievement.

To transform your dream into a goal that can be achieved, you MUST have a date for its achievement. How do you choose the date? As you've probably heard before, most people overestimate what they can do in a decade and underestimate what they can do in a year.

The goal achievement process works like a farmer planting a crop. When you picked your B.U.D., you chose the seed you would plant. Once that seed is planted, you will water the crop and tend to it until it is ready to harvest.

The major difference between achieving your goals and harvesting a crop is that the farmer knows almost exactly WHEN the crop will be ready to harvest. Each seed has what we call a gestation period. This is the time that elapses from when it is planted until when it is harvested. Your goals have a gestation period, also, but unfortunately as humans, we have never figured out the exact gestation period for a goal to grow into physical reality. <u>What we must do is take our best guess at the approximate gestation period for harvesting our goals.</u>

To do this, choose the date when you WANT to achieve your goal, even if you're not too sure at this point you CAN achieve your goal by that time. Choosing when you WANT to achieve your goal (within reason, of course- don't be ridiculous and say you want to have a billion dollars in your pocket by tomorrow morning) keeps you from giving yourself too much time to harvest your crop. If you have too much time, it will lessen your incentive to work on your farm, and therefore, there is a good chance your crops will rot before you harvest your fields.

> *It's like a farmer who sits around thinking, "Oh, yes, those crops will take five years to grow so there's no need to water them today. I can always go do it tomorrow." What the farmer failed to realize is that his entire time frame for the crop was way off. He thinks his crop will take five years to mature. Actually, his crop, if properly cared for, would be ready to harvest this fall. Since he keeps putting off the action he needs to take, his crop will end up shriveling in the field and he will never realize the joy and abundance of a healthy harvest.*

3. Give your POG some BAMS.

The next key to transforming your dream into a proper goal is to give it some BAMS. BAMS stands for **Believable, Achievable, Measurable, and Specific.**

First, **you must Believe it's possible to achieve your goal.** Notice I said, YOU must believe it. It doesn't matter what anyone else thinks, but if you don't sincerely believe that it is at least possible to achieve your goal, you will never consistently take the actions and develop the awareness necessary to turn it into reality.

Your goal must also be achievable. If you can never attain your goal, it would be pretty hard to stay motivated to work towards it don't you think? If you won't keep working toward it until you achieve it, there's no reason to even bother setting it in the first place. That is why perfection is not a goal. You could work your butt off from now until kingdom come and you would never achieve perfection.

Don't phrase your goal as "I have become the best dancer in the world." No matter how good you are, you can always get better. Therefore, you will never achieve your goal. Besides, how would you ever know if you were the best dancer? Who decides that- you, your audience, the press? What criteria do they use? How can you rank every dancer in the world? You don't even know how to list all the dancers in the world, much less figure out which ones are better or worse than you.

Next, **make sure your goal is measurable.** If you cannot measure your goal, you will never know if you achieved it. "I have become financially independent" is not measurable. Does financially independent mean a $1,000,000 net worth, a $20,000 a year income from investments, a $250,000 a year residual income or marrying a rich wife? The process for achieving all three may be quite different, so you will never know exactly what to do next to achieve your goal.

This is why you learned earlier that states of being such as "happiness" or "peace" are not goals. There is no way for you to measure them and decide in some objective manner whether you have achieved them or not.

> *Can you imagine putting together a plan of action to "be happy" and saying, "OK, I've taken steps one, two, and three. Now I'm exactly 57% of the way to happiness.*
>
> *If I just do these three things for the next 90 days, I'll be 92.4% of the way there and then by the end of the year, by golly, I'll be happy."*
>
> Not.
>
> *It doesn't work that way.*

You can only be happy or peaceful now, in the present moment. You either are experiencing happiness or peace now, or you are not. Period.

Last, **your goal must be specific** so that you know exactly what images to plant into your subconscious and so that your mind and emotions can help you choose the proper actions for achieving your goal. Don't say, "I have become financially independent." That is not specific. Say, "I have earned $1,000,000." That is specific and you can get a firm grasp on what it takes to achieve your goal.

You are designing your game of life here, so don't put rules into it that guarantee you are going to lose. Give yourself a chance. Give your goal some BAMS. Make your goal Believable, Achievable, Measurable, and Specific.

4. Make your goal harmonious.

The final key to transforming your dream into a true goal is to make it harmonious with the natural laws of the universe and your own beliefs and values. This is why you invested so much time at the start of this book in learning about the natural laws and studying your values and beliefs. If you skipped this step, you are in danger of wasting your life going after goals that either cannot be achieved or cannot be achieved without violating some of your most important beliefs and values. I hardly think that would be a good way to waste your life.

Do you?

Let's look at a few examples.

> Even though it is very specific and measurable and you can easily set a date you would like to achieve it, saying your goal is to jump off a cliff and fly for 500 miles without any kind of extra flying apparatus is not going to cut it. There's this wonderful little natural law called gravity that you are trying to violate and I hardly think you would like to spend the rest of your life fighting all the forces of nature to try to achieve a goal that is in total conflict with the world around you.
>
> Another stupid goal is to say, "I have earned $1,000,000 in the next 30 days without working." This, too, violates the natural law of sowing and reaping.

If you do not sow the seeds and do the work, you will not reap the rewards.

You will not be able to achieve goals that violate this principle. It is reversing cause and effect. The reward is the effect. The proper thought process and set of actions is the cause. You cannot get an effect without having a cause and you cannot reverse cause and effect. **Cause always precedes effect, so don't try to reverse it.**

<u>Once you know that your goal is in harmony with natural laws, be sure it is in harmony with your own beliefs and values.</u> If your top value is spending time with your family at home, be careful of setting a goal to be a professional speaker. Most professional speakers log a couple hundred days of travel time each year and that leaves very little time to spend with your family. On the other hand, it is possible to be a professional speaker who

has her audiences come to her, so don't totally eliminate the goal because it conflicts with a value like this. Just be creative about re-phrasing it and re-thinking it so that you can achieve it without violating any of your personal beliefs.

In this case, it would be perfectly acceptable to re-phrase your goal to say, "I have touched 100,000 people with my direct spoken message without traveling more than 30 days out of the year." Then, in the next step you would focus on speaking only to large audiences, getting your audiences to come to you, or focusing on local groups to reach your goal of touching 100,000 people without traveling more than 30 days.

You now know all the **keys for transforming your Big Ultimate Dream into your Primary Overall Goal:**

1. Write it in present tense.
2. Give yourself a date for achieving it.
3. Make it believable, attainable, measurable, and specific.
4. And make it harmonious with natural laws and your beliefs and values.

Write your Primary Overall Goal here:

_____

Checklist for evaluating your Primary Goal:
Now, evaluate your goal with this checklist:

- *Is my goal written in present tense?*
- *Have I chosen a date for achieving it?*
  - *Have I given myself enough, but not too much, time to achieve it?*
- *Is my goal believable, specific, measurable, and achievable?*
- *Is my goal in harmony with natural laws?*
- *Does my goal match my beliefs and values?*
  Congratulations.

You are ready to complete your Stress-Free Success Plan.

Lesson 12:
Develop And Execute An Effective Daily Stress-Free Success Plan

"Your Stress-Free Success Plan"

If you have never set any goals before, the process that you just went through to set your goal may seem like a lot of work. Think of it in these terms, though, and you will realize that it is really not too bad:

- You are directing your own life here. Isn't it worth a little effort to make your life the life of a champion instead of a loser?

- Add up the hours you spent planning the last major project you worked on - maybe a presentation to a key client, designing the addition on your home, or the preparation for your daughter's wedding. You put in quite a bit of time and effort didn't you? And that was only for a small portion of your life. This is for the whole ball of wax.

- The planning process that you just completed is like the offseason preparation that a coach and his staff goes through to get ready for next year. If you've ever been involved with athletics, you know that a championship season is a year-round affair. The coaches invest almost as much time and energy preparing for the season as they do coaching the season when it occurs.

Get ready to coach your team to "Your Gold Medal Season" of goal achievement.

Here are the steps you will follow:

The 6 Steps To Developing A Daily Stress-Free Success Plan

1. Let go of the past and forget your previous losses
2. Improve your focus by eliminating distractions
3. Shed the extra pounds of false beliefs
4. Eliminate your fears
5. Harness the power of the unseen forces to help you succeed
6. Complete your Stress-Free Daily Success Plan

Are you ready to coach yourself to victory?

May the games begin...

Step #1: Let go of the past

The first key to this phase of Stress-Free Success is to let go of the past. **The past does not determine your future.** Today is the first day of your new season of life. It is a blank slate and you can fill it with whatever you choose. As the manager of your own team, you will choose success. Address these areas first:

• **The past does not determine the future.** In the natural order of the world, your actions create the future that you will experience. Since you are free to act and think any way you would like, you are free to create any future you would like, no matter what happened in the past. Just because you failed at something in the past does not mean that you cannot succeed at it in the future. From 1962 to 1968, the New York Mets had one of the most abysmal records ever recorded in the hundreds years of professional baseball. In fact, in 1968 the Mets finished ninth out of ten teams in the National League. Just one year later, they were sitting on top of the world after stunning the Baltimore Orioles in the World Series. You can turn your life around in the same way - IF you commit to developing and executing a workable plan.

• **What must you stop doing, even though you do it very well, in order to succeed at the particular**

goal you have chosen? Let's say you are one of the world's best writers and you usually write for eight hours each day. Your goal is to win an Olympic gold medal in gymnastics. You must quit (or at least not spend so much time) writing to give yourself the time you need to improve your gymnasatics skills to the world-class level. Unless you have a super-human ability to stay focused, you will be hard-pressed to also invest enough quality hours in practicing your gymnastics skills, if you continue to invest eight hours a day in writing.

In the business world, the same analogy is true.

Let's say you are an expert accountant. Your goal is to build a publishing business that you can sell for $500,000 within two years. If you invest all your time in accounting, you will not have enough left to invest in the higher-level entrepreneurial thinking skills that are necessary to build a business that quickly. Even though you are good at it, delegate the accounting to someone else so that you can invest in the activities that are the highest and best use of your time.

Legend has it that Frank Sinatra was excellent at giving up the things that did not move him closer to his goal. One of my favorite quotes **is "Frank Sinatra doesn't move pianos.**" This doesn't mean that he was vain or thought he was too good to do manual labor, it just means that he understood that his fame and fortune rested on his singing ability, not his ability to get the stage ready for him to sing.

He did what he did best and allowed others to do the rest.

You should do the same.

• **What would a superstar do?** To figure out what activities are the highest and best use of your time, ask yourself, what would a superstar do? **Do the same things that the best people in your field do.**

Michael Jordan shot thousands of jump shots to become the world's best basketball player. Jack Nicklaus made thousands of chip shots, putts, and drives to take his golf game to a world-class level. Martina Navralitova smashed thousands of serves across the net to win her tennis championships. Bill Gates invested thousands of hours in developing software and marketing strategies to make Microsoft a world-class computer company and himself one of the world's youngest billionaires.

These people are all world-class performers, but they were not born that way. They practiced the right activities relentlessly in order to take their games to the highest level. Do the same for your game. **Do what the superstars do.**

Step #2: Improve your focus by eliminating distractions

Once you have cleaned your slate by letting go of the past, you are ready to sharpen your focus on your goal by eliminating distractions from your life.

In the case of goal-achieving**, anything that does not move you closer to your goal is a distraction** that must be given up or eliminated.

If your goal is to win an Olympic gold medal, winning the Nobel Prize is a distraction.

If your goal is to build a successful business, winning an Olympic medal is a distraction.

> *Analyze your weekly activities. How many of them contribute directly to your primary overall goal? How many of them do not?*

One of the primary sources of distractions for most of us is our thoughts. We waste hundreds of hours a year thinking about political issues, the weather, and other people's business. Not only can we can do nothing about them, they distract us from achieving our goals as well. If the issue won't affect you in ten years, don't worry about it now. Give it up and get on with creating your perfect life.

While we're on the subject of giving things up, add petty disagreements to your list.

> *How many hours in the past five years have you wasted in petty disagreements that when you look back on them now, had no real lasting effect on your life? How much farther ahead would you be if you had invested all those hours in pursuing your dream?*

As Edie Brickell sings, "Nothing keeps me up all night. I toss and turn over nothing. Nothing can cause a great big fight."

But only if you let it.

So don't.

Notice that you're fighting about nothing before nothing become something - and something becomes insurmountable.

> *If you really feel like you need to vent all your frustrations and built-up emotions, try this: give yourself ten minutes a day to go nuts with them. Rant, rave, yell, scream, cuss, cry, or whatever you want to do.*
>
> *There are only two caveats:*
>
> *1. <u>You have to record yourself doing it</u>.*
>
> *2. And, when you're done, <u>you have to play it back</u> and ask yourself, "Are those problems really worth getting worked up all over? Is it worth giving up pursuing my dream just to argue over stupid little stuff like that?"*
>
> *Another way to approach your 10-minute session is to tease yourself. Act as if you are your own most sarcastic friend.*
>
> *Say, "Ooooooh, poor baby, did you cut your little finger today? Ooooooh, that's too bad. You must have a really terrible life.*

Maybe you should go pout about it for a while, you selfish little clod of ailments, you."

Record that tirade, play it back, and I will almost guarantee you that you have no trouble giving up most of your minor frustrations and distractions in the future.

Did you know that Michael Jordan, Pete Rose, Bill Gates, Ross Perot, and Arnold Schwartzenegger are some of the laziest people in the world? In fact, they are usually <u>fanatically lazy - fanatically lazy about doing anything that does not contribute to their goals</u>.

And fanatically obsessed about staying focused on those things that do contribute toward their goals.

Develop the same habit in yourself.

It works.

Very well.

Step #3: Shed the extra pounds of false beliefs

Many of the beliefs you hold (or hopefully at this point, you held) do not contribute to the achievement of your goals. <u>Keeping these beliefs is like lugging a "spare tire" around your middle. They slow you down and keep you from performing at your best, so you must get rid of them</u> in order to allow yourself to move smoothly to world-class goal-achiever status.

Since we already addressed many of the common false beliefs and false paradigms earlier, there is no need to go into depth on them here.

What you need to do **is go back to your list of core beliefs and carefully think about each of them.**

Does the belief contribute to the achievement of your primary goal or does it hold you back from achieving your goal?

Get rid of any beliefs that hold you back by replacing them with a new, more productive belief. Notice that I said, "<u>replacing</u>" them.

Beliefs are just like habits. You get rid of old beliefs by replacing them with new ones. Once the new belief has been conditioned, it becomes a natural part of your new, goal-achiever make-up.

Go through each area of your life and follow the same line of thinking.

> *Do my beliefs in this area help me reach my goals or do they slow me down?*

Step #4: Eliminate your fears

> *"Fear and doubt knocked on the door. Faith and courage answered. There was no one there." Old proverb*

It is common at this point to be feeling a sense of fear deep down inside you - a feeling that you're not so sure you CAN make these changes in your life and a sense that you're not too sure you WANT to invest all the time and energy it sometimes requires to turn your dreams into reality.

> *That's normal, so don't worry about it.*

> *After all, you're growing. Growth involves stepping boldly into the unknown. And the unknown is often a bit scary.*

> *If you DIDN'T feel that way, you'd need to start worrying because you probably wouldn't be growing.*

So, let's go back to those feelings of doubt and fear eating away at your insides.

First, there's no question that <u>you CAN do anything you set your mind to</u>. You are an expression of infinite spirit and when you put the power of the natural laws of the universe on your side, you will achieve breakthroughs you didn't think were possible.

To overcome your fears, remember these points...
Fear is a sign you're growing.

If you don't feel fear on a daily basis, you are in your comfort zone. You know that it's impossible to grow if you stay in your comfort zone all the time. **Rejoice in your fear because it is a healthy response from your body telling you that you are experiencing growth.**

Fear comes when the thoughts and images you are placing into your subconscious are in conflict with the images and conditioning that is already there. Each time you feel your fear, just tell yourself, *"I understand that I am feeling fear because the new thoughts that I am having are creating a conflict in my subconscious. This is good. This means that I am re-programming my subconscious and growing into more of my potential as a wonderful human being."*

Cross your 'terror barrier' by telling yourself, *"I am making a conscious decision to take action based on the new thoughts that I am having. This action is helping me to grow and I am joyful for the opportunity to grow in this way."*

Then take action toward whatever it is that scares you. And have fun doing it.

We learn our fears, so we can unlearn them.

Fears are conditioned responses to your environment. You were born practically fearless. The only fears that most babies are born with are the fear of falling and fear of loud noises. Virtually every single other fear develops later as a response to events in your life. If your fears are a product of your conditioning, you have the capability to "unlearn" them the same way that you learned them in the first place.

Ask yourself, *"Why do I believe I can't do this thing?"*

"Pluck your brain out" and examine it from a distance.

Ask,

"Is there a rational reason for the belief?

Could I be mistaken in the belief?

Why do I continue to act and feel this fear

What is the worst thing that could happen to me if I went ahead and did the thing that I am scared of?

If it is within your moral and legal bounds, go out and do it, just for the heck of it. Go into it with an attitude of discovery.

View the whole process as one of discovery. You are discovering why you think and act the way you do. You are discovering more about yourself and the world around you. You are discovering the limits of your potential. You are discovering how just how much fun it can be to test those limits and overcome your fears.

Enjoy!

You are separate from your fears.

By writing down a list of your fears, you have already taken one of the biggest steps to overcoming them. You are now conscious of your fears and realize that your fears are separate from you. Don't be afraid to look at yourself and figure out where your fears come from and why you have them. Realize that deep inside of you is a perfectly spiritual being that is independent of all your conditioned fears. Getting in touch with this inner core of your being is a totally liberating experience and you WILL like what you find in there.

You must release the old to make room for new

Which would motivate you more: the chance to earn $1,000,000 in the next year or the opportunity (or necessity) to keep from losing the $1,000,000 that you earned last year? Almost all of us would say we would be more motivated to work to keep from losing the $1,000,000 we already had than to gain the $1,000,000 we hadn't yet earned. That means <u>for most of us the fear of loss is stronger than the potential of gain.</u>

If we live our lives with this hierarchy of beliefs, we will waste most of our lives and tie up virtually all our energy trying to hold onto the things we think we already have.

This is dangerous for two reasons:

First, we don't already have any physical things because physical things are all temporary. Trying to hold on to them is like trying to run in quicksand. We'll never feel too secure inside if we try to do it.

Second, if we're investing our time and energy into holding on to what we already have - material things, belief systems, relationships, and all the rest - we won't have a whole lot of time or energy left over for pursuing what we really want.

Think about that for a minute. If you are trying to hold on to what you already have, you are guaranteeing that you'll never get what you really want. You have to let go of one to get the other.

Think of this process as a spring cleaning. You want some new clothes. Your closet is full of old clothes. Until you clean out the closet and get rid of the old clothes that don't work for your anymore, you won't have any room for the new one.

Begin your own spring cleaning. Begin releasing all of the things in your life that are holding you back. Release your limiting values, beliefs, and the physical possessions that are not totally ideal for you. Get ready for a burst of energy that you will feel as you free up your resources from holding on to the old.

Those people you are closest to often want you to keep your fears

Often times those people we are closest to do the sabotage our dreams and help us to keep our fears. Usually, these people are suffering from some form of low self-esteem. They are afraid themselves that if we are successful and overcome our fears, we'll "move on" and leave them behind. They do not want to "lose" us, so they try to hold us back to their own level. Ignore them.

> *The best thing that you can do for yourself and for them is to become a shining example of a self-aware human being who is overcoming fears daily and realizing more and more of the potential and goodness inside.*

These people do not "need" you and they will not "lose" you because there is no way they can possess you in the first place. Their entire paradigm is flawed if they think this way. You could tell them this, but usually our helpful ideas will fall on deaf ears and they may even be met with ridicule or scorn. Become independent of them.

You only live once. Live your life the way you want and play your game by YOUR rules. If they truly care about you, they will respect you. And, if you keep an open-minded, loving attitude toward them, they will realize that you do in fact still care about them and they will eventually begin to follow your lead down the path of growth.

Never compromise the rules of your game. Stick to what you believe and work daily to overcome your fears and live your life on a higher level.

Do your daily work with the joyful attitude **that the more successful you are, the more people you will be able to help**. Rejoice in the fact that as you succeed and more windows of opportunity open to you, you will be able to reach out to your friends and loved ones and "bring them along for the ride," not by giving them money or things, but by giving them opportunities to earn money and to grow and learn more about themselves.

And that is the most wonderful gift you can ever give.

Step #5: Recruit TUF, your secret weapon

It's now time for you to recruit your own "secret weapon" for goal achievement, a Hall of Fame legend named TUF. **In the language of goal achievement,**

TUF means "The Unseen Forces" - in other words, the power of your subconscious mind and the other unseen forces that are operating around you constantly.

In order to get TUF to work for you, you must now follow three steps:

1. Picture your goal in the present
2. Solidify the goal's image in your mind
3. Turn the perfected image over to The Unseen Forces, and let them run with it

Let's look at each in order:

Picture your goal in the present

We have already discussed the importance of thinking of your goal in the present tense, as if you already have your goal in physical reality. As you know, your mind deals only with the present - it does not recognize past or future tense. Imagining you in possession of your goal in the present strengthens the connection between your conscious, subconscious, and your body and allows all of the forces at your command to begin working in harmony.

Start practicing this now.

Close your eyes and let your imagination run free. Loosen the limits on your thinking. Gently relax all of the muscles in your body. Let your abdomen sag and your jaw drop.

> *What does it feel like to have achieved your goal? What do you look like standing with possession of your goal? What are the sounds, smells, and sights around you? What emotions are you experiencing? Who else is in the picture? What do they think of you? What do they do to congratulate you on achieving your goal?*

To make this process easier and more effective, **get a symbol to represent your goal.** One of the best ways to do this is to take a picture of you with your goal.

If your goal is a new Mercedes, go down to your local dealership and snap a couple photos of you sitting in the Mercedes or standing proudly next to it. If your goal is a new house, find a house like the one you would like and take your picture standing in front of it. You can get really creative with this as well. If your goal is to build a successful mail order business, go down to the post office and see if they'll let you have your picture taken with a bag of mail that symbolizes all the orders you are receiving. If your goal is to travel to Italy, you could get a slide or overhead transparency of Italy, project it on the wall, and have your picture taken in front of it, so it looks like you are part of the scene.

With today's color scanners, it's also easy to scan a photo of you and a photo of your goal and then merge them in the computer so they can be printed out in a full-color composite image.

<u>Another excellent symbol of your goal is a goal card.</u> Get a blank business card or cut some paper or card stock into that size. Write your Primary Overall Goal on the card and carry it with you everywhere. You might want to laminate the card, and it would probably be even more effective to put a picture of you with your goal on one side of the card and the written description of your goal on the other side.

Mark Victor Hansen, author of *Chicken Soup for the Soul* and one of the most joyous and prosperous people I've ever met, suggests that you carry a $100 bill wrapped around your goal card to remind you of the prosperity that is now part of your life. That's an excellent idea.

> *If your goal is monetary in nature, go down to the bank and get a blank check register book. Record your weekly or monthly deposits from the income you will be earning and record your net balance at the end of your goal-achievement period.*

For example, if your goal is to earn $180,000 this year, record a deposit of $15,000 on the first of each month. Increase your balance each month until it reaches $180,000 in December. You can do the same thing with a few blank tax returns. Change the date on the tax return to the appropriate year and record the income you will earn this year

<u>Whatever symbol you choose, display it prominently where you will see it on a regular basis.</u> You may even want to get copies made and place one in your office, one on the refrigerator, and one near your bed. The idea is to keep building a clearer and clearer image of you in possession of your goal and the pictures help you do that.

> As your image gets clearer, it's like wiping mud off a pair of glasses. The cleaner you get the lens, the easier it is to see where you're going. The clearer your goal-achieving image is, the easier it is to see which direction you must go to achieve it. Pick a regular time each day and practice visualizing yourself in possession of your goal.

Your Dream Book Revisited

Take a few minutes now and insert pages in your Dream Book or Book of Perfect Life that you created earlier for each of the aspects of your ideal life - your image of you in possession of your goal, a written description of your goal, pictures of other things you would like to do, see, or experience, people you would like to meet, your personal creed, core beliefs, and mission statement, and anything else that you would like to include.

Solidify your goal's image in your mind

Picturing your goal in the present and getting a symbol to represent your goal gave you a good basic image to work with. The next step is to solidify that image. <u>The image is the blueprint for a bridge between where you are and where you want to be.</u> Solidifying the image is like building the bridge from your blueprint. The better the blueprint, the stronger the bridge that you will build. The stronger the bridge that you build, the easier and quicker your team can cross into the land of your ideal life.

You have already engaged the power of your eyes and the written word in this process. Now you will add the power of the spoken word.

Get a blank cassette tape and put it into a cassette player that will record. Record your written description of your Primary Overall Goal in your own voice on the cassette. Use personal pronouns ("I", not "you"), speak in the present tense, and make your description short, specific and concise.

Then record a description of what it feels like to have achieved your goal - the sights, sounds, smells, and emotions that you are experiencing. Make your descriptions as vivid and real as possible. Imagine that you are an Academy Award winning actor portraying you in a screen play of your life. Get into the role. Laugh, yell, cry, giggle, or whatever seems appropriate to really describe your goal.

You may even want to play some music such as the theme from "Rocky" or the William Tell Overture in the background. The point is, you must get emotionally involved with your goal in order for you to be able to connect with all the unseen forces that are available to you. Recording your goal in this manner helps you develop an intense emotional desire to achieve your goal and it solidifies in your mind the image of you having already achieved your goal.

After you record your goal and your description of what it is like to have achieved your goal, record your commitment to visualize your goal-achieving image daily. Say something like, "I know that visualization is the key to unlocking the power inside of me and I enjoy visualizing my goal and listening to this cassette daily."

Then complete your cassette by recording your focus or mission statement, your core beliefs, your values, and your personal creed.

Turn your perfected image over to TUF and let him run with it

You have developed a perfected image of you in possession of the goal you have set. You have consciously thought about your goal, and you have used your faculties of sight and hearing to help solidify the image of your goal in your mind on a conscious level.

Now it's time to turn your perfected image over to your "secret weapon," TUF. Remember, **TUF stands for "The Unseen Forces." TUF is all of the power that lies latent inside of you and the universe around you.** Through TUF, you will attract to you the resources and circumstances that are necessary to achieve your goal.

Remember, too, TUF is your superstar. He NEVER fails, and he ALWAYS wins the game for you. That's why it's so important to have him on your team.

Since TUF is such a powerful ally, there is a special process for turning your perfected image over to him and enlisting his support for your cause. You have completed the first step of this process by making written, visual, and verbal descriptions of your goal.

The second step is to turn your image over to the part of TUF that lies in your subconscious mind. You do this by relaxing and consciously imagining the image of you in possession of your goal. You then use your conscious mind to imagine yourself creating a duplicate of your image in your subconscious - that is, you "turn your image over to your subconscious."

Here is what happens when you do this:

1. You started with your conscious mind becoming involved with the image of your goal.

2. You then created a duplicate of this image in your subconscious by "turning the image over" to your subconscious.

3. This image will help you become emotionally involved with your goal. As your thoughts and emotions change, you will become in

harmony with all of the resources in the universe that you need to achieve your goal.

4. This harmonious vibration will attract these resources to you.

As **Genevieve Behrend** says in Your Invisible Power, *"When your understanding grasps the power to visualize your heart's desire and holds it with your will, it attracts to you all things requisite to the fulfillment of that picture, by the harmonious vibrations of the law of attraction... Visualizing is the great secret of success."*

Since your body is the physical instrument that the images in your mind are expressed through, you will know what actions are appropriate to take to efficiently use these resources to smoothly and naturally create a physical manifestation of your goal.

By following this process on a daily basis, you are 2/3 of the way to achieving your goal. You already possess your goal on the conscious and subconscious levels. The only thing left is to create it on the physical level. Let's put together a game *plan to help you do just that.*

Step #6: Develop your Stress-Free Success Plan

"If you can do half of something, you can do the whole thing." John Noe, author of Peak Performance P**rinciples for High Achievers**

To develop a simple, but powerful plan for achieving your goal, answer these questions:

- **What 3-6 actions, if done daily, will move you the furthest and quickest toward your goal?**
- *What is the* **first step** *you must take to reach your goal?*
- *What are the* **next steps**?
- *What are the* **milestones** *that will tell you you are on the right track?*

- What **rewards** will you receive along the way?
- **Who will you be accountable to** for the actions you need to take to achieve your goal?
- **How will you schedule your time** for maximum goal-achievement effectiveness?

Those questions may sound simple, but they are critically important. <u>This is the area where most would-be goal-achievers fall short.</u> They go through all this work to set their goals and then they rush out to set the world on fire. The problem is, they don't have an effective plan and soon they are either frustrated from their lack of progress or confused because they seemed incredibly busy for the past few months and didn't move any closer to their goal.

Let's examine each of these questions in more depth so that you won't make the same mistakes.

What 3-6 actions, if done daily, will move you the furthest and quickest toward your goal?

What you are looking for here is <u>the important, but not necessarily urgent, activities.</u>

> *For example, when I decided to write this book, I had two daily activities that I knew I must do to complete it in 90 days or less: first, write 2000 words daily; second, invest one hour in writing ad copy and developing marketing ideas to sell it.*
>
> *That was it.*
>
> *I knew if I do those two things everything else would come together and the book would be finished. I also knew that in order to be able to do those two things, I would naturally have had to take all the other steps such as research and outlining that led up to the writing and marketing. Therefore, by "kerchunking" my goal down to two manageable, daily tasks, I was writing a guarantee for myself that I would get the book done.*

Another good example is Rusty Jones, a salesperson who set a goal to earn $100,000 in commissions this year, or about double what he did last year. His critical daily actions were making phone contact with at least 20 prospects, setting at least 3 appointments, and investing one hour in practicing his presentation. He knew that if he made daily contact with 20 prospects, was face to face with at least three of them, and became an expert at his presentation, he would sell enough prospects to achieve his goal.

Here are a few examples of the potential key activities for different types of goals:

Sales goals: contacting 20 prospects by phone, setting 5 appointments, closing one sale, practicing your presentation for one hour, or mailing 500 lead generation letters

Entrepreneurial goals: sending samples to 10 new potential distributors, contacting 3 other successful business owners to share ideas, investing one hour in walking the shop floor to talk to employees, investing one hour in reading relevant trade journals and personal development books, or investing two hours in training your employees.

Athletic goals: running 5 miles, shooting 100 free throws, making 100 putts, hitting 100 pitches, or investing one hour in lifting weights.

Health goals: eating less than 20% of your calories from fat, eating less than 3000 calories, eating at least 5 servings of fruit or vegetables, or working out for at least 30 minutes.

Personal goals: investing one hour in quality time with your family, telling your spouse and kids you love them at least once, sincerely complimenting at least one of your friends or family members, listening to your spouse share their feelings for at least 30 minutes, meditating for 20 minutes, visualizing for 30 minutes.

Notice a couple things about these examples:

- *They are simple*
- *They are tasks that move you toward your goal in the quickest manner possible*
- *They are specific and measurable*

You are looking for the few critical areas that will vault you toward your goal. Usually these areas are very easy to understand and accomplish. A golfer knows if he sinks 100 putts per day, he will lower his overall score. A salesperson knows if he contacts 20 prospects a day, he will make more sales. A parent knows if he invests one hour in listening to his kids thoughts each day, he will develop a better relationship with them.

The key thing here is that they are tasks that will move you toward your goal in the quickest possible manner. It's likely that you may realize two things when you are thinking about the critical tasks for achieving your goal:

• **The tasks may or may not be what you do well.**

Don't be afraid to admit that what you do well may not be the most important thing for achieving your goal. You could be the best phone salesperson in the world but that won't help you much if your goal is to win the Nobel Prize in physics.

That's OK.

You have infinite potential inside you and by doing the important things daily, no matter what, you will become better at them. It's just like lifting weights. The more you lift, the easier it is for your muscles to move the lighter weights.

• **The tasks may or may not be what you usually do.**

You may be used to sitting in the library doing research all afternoon, but if you want to build a million dollar business quickly, you may find that one of your critical tasks is to talk to three potential investors daily. This will require doing some things that you aren't used to doing and that you may not initially be that good at.

Do them anyway.

You overcome fear by action. You build skills with action. You grow through action.

You're like pond water. Without action, you stagnate. With action, your entire environment becomes alive with growth and prosperity, just like moving water helps the pond's ecosystem grow and prosper.

- **The tasks must be specific and measurable.**

You must be able to tell if and when you have completed your daily tasks. It does you no good to say, "I will practice jump shots today." Does "practicing" mean shooting five shots or 500?

What will it take to help you reach the level you want to perform at?

The key in this whole process is not coming up with some convoluted, complicated plan. The key is picking a handful of truly important things and doing them, day in and day out, no matter what.

No excuses. Period.

Write your top 3 daily goal-achieving actions here:

1. _____
2. _____
3. _____

Now, we are going to add a couple things that will assure you of leading an even happier, more satisfying life.

Look at the way your goal is phrased. Seriously consider adding a phrase like "while leading a healthy, balanced life" to the end of your goal. A phrase like that will keep the importance of health and balance in the forefront of your mind and will keep you from getting out-of-hand with achieving one goal to the exclusion and detriment of the other areas of your life.

If you agree that adding a phrase such as that makes sense, I would recommend filling out your daily six actions with at least one health-related activity and one other activity that will help you achieve balance in your life.

For me, I filled out my "daily half dozen" with these three activities:
- Eat healthy food with less than 20% of my calories from fat
- Exercise at least 30 minutes
- Visualize and review my goals

That last daily activity is critically important and I would strongly recommend that you make it a part of your daily actions. Visualizing and reviewing your goals helps you build stronger images in your mind which allow more of your potential and ability to rise to the surface. They also keep you focused on your goals so that you don't get side-tracked with needless activities.

This kind of exercise also strengthens your "mind muscles." Stronger "mind muscles" allow you to achieve higher goals quicker just like stronger body muscles allow you to lift heavier weights quicker.

Write your revised "daily half dozen" activities here:

1. _____
2. _____
3. _____
4. _____
5. _____
6. _____

Now, copy them onto a clean sheet of paper with the heading "I will complete these activities each day, before I go to bed. No excuses. Period."

Add these to your Dream Book and record them in your own voice on your goal-achievement cassette that you made earlier.

What is the first step?

The next question you must answer to complete your Goal Achievement Action Plan is what is the first step toward your goal.

By this time, it should be clear to you what the first step you must take is. If it is not, begin with an image of you in possession of your goal and work backwards.

What must have occurred right before you achieved your goal? What must have occurred right before that? And right before that?

Eventually, you will work your way back to the first step you must take.

I did a form of this thinking when I put together a plan for writing this book. I saw myself with the completed book in hand and said, "What must have occurred right before that?" Obviously, the book would have had to be printed. Before that, it would have had to be accepted by a publisher and edited. Before that, I would have had to write a proposal to a publisher. Before that, I would have had to write and outline the book. Since the book was already outlined, the first step that I had not yet completed was writing the book. That became my priority. I estimated that the completed book would be 120,000 words. I gave myself 12 weeks to finish it, so I knew I had to write 10,000 words per week. Working five days a week, I knew that if I wrote 2,000 words per day, I would complete the book on time.

You will not always be able to determine every single step from where you are now to where you want to be. In fact, usually you will have areas where you can only guess at what must occur. In my case, I knew that to earn $1,000,000 from the sale of this book, I would obviously need to do some serious marketing for the book.

I could not predict in advance, however, whether that would be radio talk shows, a book-signing tour, book store sales, mail order sales, or some other form of marketing. That was good, because I knew that since I couldn't predict everything in advance, my goal was big enough to stretch my imagination and cause me to grow as a person in order to reach it.

Don't let the fact that you don't know every step in advance keep you from getting started. The key is to figure out what the first step is, and leave it at that. Once you complete the first step, you will be able to see where you should go next.

As Thomas Carlyle once said, **"Go as far as you can see. When you get there, you'll see how to go farther."**

> It's like taking a walk on a foggy night. You know that you are moving forward toward the light in the distance, but you can't see all the steps along the way. You can, however, see where your next step should be.
>
> You take it.
>
> Once you do, you can see the next step, and then the next, and so on until you reach your goal.

What do you think the next step is?

The next element of your GAAP is to determine what you think the next step is. Notice that I said, "think." The funny thing about setting and achieving lofty goals that make you stretch is that you'll never know all the steps you need to take in advance. Long-term planning never works exactly the way that you want it to, but it is valuable to give you a general direction to move in. Spend as much time as you need mapping out what you think the next step is to achieve your goal.

Then outline all the subsequent steps that you think will be necessary to reach your goal. Remember, <u>HOW you are going to accomplish these steps is irrelevant at this</u>

point. You are producing a map for your goal achievement. It tells you where you need to go. It is then up to your internal navigator, the subconscious mind, to come to your aid and help you forge a smooth, clear path to get there. Go through the process of mapping the route to your goal by following the procedure we talked about earlier:

- Start with your goal and ask, "What must have been the step that occurred right before I accomplished my goal?"
- Then ask, "What must have been the step that occurred right before that?"
- Repeat this procedure until you have worked you way backwards to wherever you are starting from today.

• **What are the milestones that will tell you you are on the right track?**

Now that you have a tentative plan for achieving your goal, it is time to set up your milestones that will help you stay on track. Think of your milestones as road markers that tell you how many miles it is to your destination and allow you to tell how many miles you have come from your starting point.

<u>Break your Primary Overall Goal down into 3-10 chunks and set milestones that will tell you when you reach each.</u> For example, to write this book, I estimated that I would need to complete 100-120,000 words. That worked out to 10,000 words per week, so that was a natural milestone to keep. I also set a milestone for passing the 100,000 word mark.

If your goal is sales or money-related, you may set milestones at certain percentages of the big goal. For example, if your big goal is to earn $1,000,000 in commissions, your milestones may be $100,000, $250,000, $500,000 and $750,000.

Write your primary goal here:

_____

Write your milestones here:

1. _____
2. _____
3. _____
4. _____
5. _____

- **What rewards will you receive along the way?**

One of the most important parts of goal-achieving is enjoying the journey. If you give up all your present-moment pleasure for some elusive future vision of the utopia you will live in when you achieve your goal, you will never be happy. Even if you do achieve your goal, you will feel a fleeting bit of pleasure and then you will be empty inside once again.

Take time to smell the roses along the way by setting up a series of rewards for yourself as you reach each milestone on the way to your goal.

> *I rewarded myself with the Macintosh Powerbook 520c that I used to write this book once I completed the outline for the book. I then rewarded myself with a long, lazy weekend trip when I finished the first draft of the book and another trip when I finished editing the book.*
>
> *Along the way, I made sure that I enjoyed every moment of writing the book by sitting in the sunshine, letting the breeze come in the open windows, and taking frequent short breaks to reflect on how fortunate I am to be able to write and express myself in this way and to thank God for the blessings in my life. You can follow the same kind of process.*

Set up rewards that are meaningful to you for each milestone on the way to your goal.

If you have your heart set on a new Infiniti, buy it when you reach $250,000 in commissions. Treat yourself to a professional massage when you have successfully contacted 10 good prospects for 21 straight days. Take the afternoon off and walk in the woods to celebrate making your first $10,000 sale. Or enjoy a romantic dinner with your spouse when you have enjoyed at least one hour per day alone with your children for the past month.

Write down the rewards for each of your milestones here:

	Milestone	Reward
1.		
2.		
3.		
4.		
5.		

- **How will you schedule your time for maximum goal-achievement?**

Now that you know what you should do and who you will be accountable to for doing it, you need to develop a plan for actually doing it on a daily basis. You are developing the pattern that will allow you to weave the fabric of daily existence into a masterpiece of exquisite beauty. Each of us will have our method of accomplishing our daily tasks, but here are a few principles to remember when developing yours:

The 12 keys for making time your ally
- Key #1: **Do the important, not the urgent, first.** Schedule your "daily half dozen" activities near the beginning of the day so that you will accomplish them

when you are fresh. This will also make it less likely that they will get put off because you run out of hours in the day.

- Key #2: **Block periods of the day for a specific priority.** One powerful way to do this is to divide your week into 21 even blocks. Each day will have three blocks: morning, afternoon, and evening. Make a chart with these 21 blocks on it. Then fill in the general priority you will address during each period.

For example, your general activity in the morning block each day may be "Prospecting." You can then fill in the specific people you will call each day. Or, your general activity for the evening block on Tuesday and Thursday may be "Family time." You can then fill in the specific type of activity you will do with your family each day as you see fit. Leave at least three of the blocks open for "Relaxation and rejuvenation." Use them to meditate, review your goals, take a nap, or put your feet up and read a good book. It is also helpful to schedule one block, perhaps Wednesday or Thursday evening, for "Catchup" to do all the little tasks that you haven't had time to do the rest of the week.

"Blocking" your time in this way simplifies your life and makes it much easier to plan your goal achievement program. The principle here is to organize weekly and then adapt daily. If 21 blocks does not work for you, try adding an extra block each day around lunch or dinner time. This would be a good way to build exercise time into your program.

Once you have your general blocks filled in, don't change them. The general rule to remember is, work when you work, play when you play, and don't mix the two. If you are in a "Prospecting" block, do nothing but prospect. If you are in a "Family time" block, do nothing but spend time with your family. And enjoy the time wholeheartedly, without guilt, because you know this is part of your plan for living your ideal life.

- Key #3: **Decide on your highest priorities and have the courage to say no to everything that does not support them.** In your blocks, you have scheduled your priorities. If someone asks you to do something that does not match your priorities, politely decline the invitation and move forward on your goal-achieving activities. If something comes up that does not support one of your highest values, don't do it. **If something comes up that supports one of your lower-level goals, but does not contribute directly to your Primary Overall Goal, don't do it.**

Many of us complain that there aren't enough hours in the day to get everything done that we need to do. That simply isn't true. **We all have the exact same number of hours, and we can all choose how to invest each of them. Make a wise investment.**

Choose goal-achieving activities. Decline tension-relieving activities such as watching soap operas or exchanging gossip with the neighbors. To make these decisions about what to do, ask yourself, **"In 10 years, doing which of these activities will affect my life in the most positive manner?"**

Then do it.

Joyously and guiltlessly.

- Key #4: **Become blissfully lazy.** You probably thought all this goal-achieving stuff was hard work, didn't you? Now is your chance to become lazy - blissfully lazy - without remorse or guilt. **Become incredibly lazy at doing anything that does not contribute to living your dream.** You have 50 things you "should" be doing right now, but none of them would really make a big difference in achieving your dream?

Get lazy.

Don't do them.

Most of them will be "completed through neglect." That means that in a day or so, they won't seem so important and your life won't be negatively affected by not doing them.

• Key #5: **Delegate ruthlessly**. Every time you are considering starting a new project or activity, ask yourself, "Is this the highest and best use of my time?" If there are activities that must be done but are not the highest and best use of your time, delegate them. Here are the **keys to effective delegation**:

- Focus on results, not methods.

- Inform the person you are delegating the project to what result you desire.

- Give the person a time frame for achieving the result, let them know what guidelines you are setting, what resources are available, who they are accountable to, what the rewards are for achieving the result, and what the consequences are of not achieving the result.

- Then leave the person alone and let them figure out the best method for them to achieve the result you desire.

• Key #6: **Follow the 80/20 rule:** The 80/20 rule was named after Vilfredo Pareto, a 19th century Italian economist who said that 80% of the production will come from 20% of the producers. Since the 1800s, we have learned that the rule applies to almost all areas of life, including your daily schedule.

For most people, 20% of their activities will make 80% of the difference in the results they obtain. Figure out which activities make up your 20%. Do them and do them well. Then delegate the other 80% to people who are better suited for accomplishing those tasks than you are. This will free up all kinds of time in your schedule to really focus on important tasks that you enjoy doing. More importantly, it will free up all kinds of psychic energy that is normally drained by doing tasks you know are not the highest and best use of your time.

- Key #7: **To do more, be more.** In *Psychopictography*, Vernon Howard wrote, "The way to do more is to be more. To do something, you must first be someone." That is why we have focused so much in this book on understanding yourself and the world around you. By increasing your wisdom and understanding, you are becoming more aware of your hidden talents and abilities. Your awareness of these talents and abilities allows you to express them. As you express them, you can do more in less time and with less stress.

- Key #8: **Just do it.** The Nike slogan may not sell shoes, but it is a great motto for life. As Vernon Howard says, "Stop looking for ways to do things and just do them."

- Key #9: **Become aware of your frantic state.** Once you are aware of how you are needlessly rushing around trying to do activities that don't really contribute to achieving your goals, you will realize that there is an alternative to this state. Focusing on your "daily half dozen" and simplifying your life through "blocking" your days will allow you to establish a pattern of productive, unhurried work.

  Thoreau once said, **"As he simplifies his life, the laws of the universe will become less complex."** Your 100% focus on the activity at hand will help you get twice as much done in half the time because your energy will not be drained by negative emotions and extraneous, non-goal-achieving thoughts.

- Key #10: **Don't start your day until you have it finished.** If you sit down at your desk in the morning and don't know exactly what you will accomplish that day, you won't accomplish anything that day. Don't start your day until you have it finished means plan tomorrow's work today. Invest five or ten minutes at the end of the day outlining what you will accomplish tomorrow. This serves two important purposes.

  First, you will save time by immediately going to work on the most important tasks first thing in the morning. Second, by planning tomorrow today, you can place the thoughts of what you would like to accomplish in your subconscious and give it the entire evening to go to work to help you become aware of the best way to accomplish these things.

• Key #11: **The more you *dare* to do, the more you *can* do.** Enlarge your inner powers by reaching just beyond your current capabilities. Imagine yourself as a gymnast who wants to be able to do the splits. Each day you stretch a little more than the day before. You pull your muscles to the point where they begin to strain, and then hold them there. Gradually, you relax the muscle, knowing that it is getting more and more flexible each day. Soon, you are able to drop into the splits quickly and effortlessly. Your goal has been realized.

• Key #12: "**When in doubt, make a fool of yourself.** *There is a microscopically thin line between being brilliantly creative and acting like the most gigantic idiot on earth. So what the hell, leap.*" That quote from Cynthia Heimel says it all.

You can do it.

Just leap.

With the concepts you just learned in mind, it is now time to go back and revise your "daily half dozen" to even more closely reflect the high-level activities that will contribute most to achieving your goal.

> *In the process of focusing and simplifying your life, you may now have fewer than six daily activities that you must do. If so, that's great. Just revise the title of your life and focus on whatever number of activities you've identified as being important for living YOUR ideal life.*

As you think about your key activities, focus on identifying those things that you can do that no one else can do as well or as quickly or as brilliantly. Think about which activities will vault you toward your goal the quickest. Think about which activities will help you lead a healthy, balanced, enjoyable life along the way.

Write your revised "daily half dozen" activities here:

1. _____
2. _____
3. _____
4. _____
5. _____
6. _____

Now, copy them onto a clean sheet of paper with the heading "My daily half-dozen." Under the heading, write "I will complete these 6 activities each day, before I go to bed. No excuses. Period."

Replace the old sheet of your "daily half dozen" in your book of goals with this new sheet and record them in your own voice on your goal-achievement cassette that you made earlier.

A FREE GIFT FOR YOU before we move on:
I've discovered a series of additional strategies to help you effectively develop and execute your Stress-Free Success Plan. To share these with you, I've prepared a **Special Report titled, "Stress-Free Success: Phase Two."**

Normally, this Special Report is $10, but as a reader of this book, I'm offering it to you **FREE**, as my gift to you. I do ask, however, that you cover the $3 for shipping and handling to get the report to you.

A form for requesting your FREE Report is at the back of this book.

Lesson 13:
Execute Your Stress-Free Success Plan & Enjoy The Results

You now have an incredibly powerful game plan for achieving your goals without giving up your life. All that is left is for you to execute your game plan, fine tune your results, and enjoy the stress-free achievement of your goal.

Execute Your Daily Stress-Free Success Plan
Executing your game plan is a simple process. It involves only three main steps:

- **Complete your daily half dozen before going to bed every day**
- **When you complete one step of the plan, take another step forward to see what the next step is**
- **Complete that step and repeat the process**

That's all there is to it at this point. The key here is consistency. **If you keep doing the right things long enough, you WILL achieve your goal.**

Refine your actions to help you achieve quicker
Sporting events are won and lost by minuscule amounts. The difference between a winner and a loser is often hundredths of a second or fractions of a percent. This is called **The Razor's Edge**.

> The difference between Pete Rose, who had more hits than anyone else in baseball history, and the run-of-the-mill major leaguer is only one hit every five games. That's it. Only one extra hit every five games makes the difference between one of baseball's all-time best hitters

and a whole bunch of bench-warmers nobody's ever heard of.

The difference between a World Series ring and a last-place finish is usually about one extra victory per week. That's it. Just one extra run scored that gives you one extra victory each week and in October you are celebrating a world championship instead of downing Budweisers on the couch in your living room after suffering through a last-place season.

Your goal as the manager of your championship team is to give yourself the razor's edge that helps your superstars get that one extra hit every five games and helps your team win that one extra game per week that gives them the championship.

In order to develop that razor's edge that separates the champions from the rest of the pack, you need to do three things:

- **Build belief**
- **Build desire**
- **Model after other champions**

By harnessing the twin powers of belief and desire and modeling other successful people, you will develop the **razor's edge** that separates the winners from the losers.

- **Build your belief**

Building your belief is the first step in developing the 'razor's edge' in your goal achievement plan. **Without belief, you will never achieve your goals.**

The Bible tells us, "All things whatsoever ye ask in prayer, **believing**, ye shall receive."

By understanding how you work, what you value, what your role is in the universe, and how the natural laws of the universe work, you will develop an unshakable belief in your ability to achieve your goal.

All of us can easily believe in the things we can see and touch. The most successful of us, however, also believe in the power of those things they cannot see and touch. This **faith** in the ability of the subconscious mind to turn the invisible idea into a visible reality is what separates those who merely want to achieve from those who really do achieve.

The best test of your belief is how you act on an everyday basis. Do you prepare to succeed or prepare to fail? You will only receive what you expect. If you expect success and act like you have success, you will continue to receive success. If you expect failure and prepare for failure, you will get failure.

That is the law.

You cannot violate it.

> We have no idea as to the limits of what we can accomplish as human beings. A hundred years ago, it was inconceivable that we could fly. Today, I counted 27 jets going over my house in the space of 90 minutes.
>
> Less than a century ago, we had never heard of computers. Today, they dominate the world economy. Not a single large corporation in the world can survive without them.
>
> Just a few decades ago, we thought it was impossible for humans to run a 4:00 mile. Roger Bannister's unshakable faith proved us wrong. Since he broke the 4:00 mile mark, hundreds of runners have done the "impossible."

If you are going to doubt something, doubt your limits, not your abilities. Build your faith and your belief and by the natural laws of the universe, your goals cannot help but be realized.

Whatever mental picture, backed by faith, you hold in your conscious mind, your subconscious, as your ever dutiful servant, will bring to pass. Close your eyes, relax, and visualize yourself achieving your goal. Feel the emotions. Believe in your abilities. Trust the power of the unseen forces.

As Napoleon Hill said in *Think and Grow Rich*, **"Anything you can conceive and believe, you can achieve."**

The power of desire

The next critical component of turning your thoughts into things is desire. Desire wields a power as strong as belief in the manifestation of thoughts into things. **You can believe something all you want, but if you don't fuel your belief with the power of desire, you will never be able to guarantee that your thoughts turn into things.** At times, you may be able to succeed in accomplishing a goal or seeing one of your dreams turn into reality, but these times will be random. You will not be able to predict them with any certainty.

Harnessing the power of desire gives you the certainty to predict that what you truly want will manifest into your life. Think of your desires as arising from the potentialities inside of you. If this is true, then you will never have a true desire that cannot be fulfilled. You may have a wish or a thought that is not fulfilled, but you will never have a sincere desire that cannot be fulfilled.

How do you distinguish the two?

A true desire is one that you get emotionally involved in. It is one that really "juices" you up, not just for a few hours or a few day, but for the long-term. It is one that you get excited thinking about when you're all alone. It doesn't take a bunch of other people doing a "rah-rah" session to get you pumped about a true desire. It comes from deep inside of you and you sense that its manifestation will be an expression of your unique talents and potential as a wonderful human being.

Most importantly, a true desire is one in which you are willing to take action to manifest it. You can sit around all day and dream about having a new Mercedes, but that's all it is - a mere daydream. A new Mercedes becomes a true desire when you get emotionally involved in it - when you can see and touch and feel yourself in the Mercedes tooling down the road with the wind blowing in your face - before you ever own the care. When you are willing to invest a minimum of a few hours each week taking actions that will lead to the fulfillment of your desire.

If you don't get emotionally involved in your desire and aren't willing to take action to manifest it in physical reality, it is not a true desire. It is a daydream.

Enjoy it as a passing fancy and then let it go.

If you do get emotionally involved with the idea and are willing to take action to manifest it, congratulations. You are harnessing the incredible power of desire.

Desire focuses your mind on one goal and streamlines the images being formed in your subconscious mind so that all of the power of your mind and universal intelligence are working together to gather the resources necessary for the manifestation of your desire. **Once you have a true desire, you will feel focused and clear about your objective.**

The next thing for you to do is **release your attachment to a particular manifestation of your desire.** This is what the Buddha probably meant when he said to practice non-attachment. You are not becoming totally desireless. In fact, you are doing the exact opposite. You are building your desire into a clearly focused goal. What you are doing is becoming totally unattached to a particular manifestation of your desire. If you remain attached to a particular manifestation, you are limiting your mind and infinite intelligence.

Don't do it.

Let go of your attachment to a particular outcome and trust in the power of the universe to attract the resources you need for the perfect expression of your desire.

How to build desire

Over the course of the long season from the time you set your goal until you achieve it, you will face many obstacles and setbacks. Often, you will not be sure which direction to go or what to do. In the face of these challenges, your desire to achieve your goal will keep you moving forward.

Wallace Wattles once said that **"Desire is the effort of the unexpressed possibility within you, attempting to express itself through you in physical form."**

> Years ago, a young man asked Socrates how he could get wisdom. Socrates told him, "Come with me." He led the young man to a river, where he pushed the boy's head under the water, held it there until the lad was choking for air, then released him and looked into his eyes. When the young man caught his breath, Socrates asked him, "What did you desire most when you were under water?"
>
> "I wanted air," the young man said.
>
> Socrates told him, "When you want wisdom as much as you wanted air, you will receive it."

That is true desire.

How much do you want what you want? Do you want it bad enough to do whatever it takes to get it? Are you willing to give up everything else to get it, as the boy would have gladly done to get air when his head was immersed in the water?

The stronger your desire, the easier it will be to achieve your goal. As your desire increases, the forces of the universe will move in harmony with your desire and your goal will turn into physical reality.

You build your desire through a regular program of visualization and dream-building. Visualization stamps the images of you successfully achieving your goal on the blank slate of your subconscious mind. Your subconscious then goes to work to help you achieve those goals.

Psychologists tell us that **your mind cannot distinguish between a vividly imagined experience and a real experience. It reacts to both in the same way.**

This is a key point in building your desire. By visualizing yourself in possession of your goal, you are programming your future by creating memories in your mind of you achieving your goal. Since your mind will have the stamped image of you having achieved your goal, it will naturally cause you to do, say, talk and act as if you have achieved your goal. If you do those things that a goal-achiever would do, talk and think as a goal-achiever would talk and think, and act as a goal-achiever would act, you will become the goal-achiever in physical reality that you already are in your mental reality.

As you develop your desire to achieve your goal, you will feel what you should do next.

Do it.

Feeling is the language of the subconscious mind. Do what your feelings tell you to do. Follow your intuition. "Feel" your way to your goal one step at a time, just like an explorer moving through a dense forest at night.

Don't be an "almost" that just misses getting a promotion, just misses winning the game, just misses qualifying for the mortgage, and just misses living a happy life. Be a "most" that achieves the goals you set for yourself. Develop your desire through visualization and achieve your goals through the power of intuition. Trust the powers inside you.

Track your results
"When you coast, you soon roll to a stop."

"Momentum preserves energy."

You have a concise, powerful game plan. You have mastered the basics; you have recruited the unseen forces to play for you; you are managing like a champion; you are winning games left and right. Now the only thing left is for you to check the scorecard and see just how well you are doing.

Without a scorecard, you could think you are losing when you are really winning. Or you could think you are winning when you are really losing. The scorecard allows you to measure your progress and see just where you stand. It also serves as your guidepost to refining your behaviors so that you can achieve your goal even quicker and more easily.

Follow these principles when designing your goal-achievement scorecard:

• **Only compare your goals and your progress to YOUR own benchmarks.** What others can do or have done should not matter to you. You are uniquely different than every other person that has ever walked the earth. No one else has the same set of talents, abilities, values, and beliefs as you. Therefore, you cannot accurately compare yourself against anyone else. To do so would be to fall into the classic "comparing apples to oranges" trap.

Don't do it.

• **Be selfish of your time.** The ancient philosopher Theophrastus once said, "Time is the most valuable thing a man can spend."

More accurately in today's world, **"Time is the most valuable thing a man or woman can invest."** Two of the best investments of your time are a few minutes given to planning and a few minutes given to quiet contemplation of your goals and relaxation from your daily activities. Make both a regular part of your day.

Time given to thought is the greatest time-saver of them all. It keeps you from wasting your precious moments frantically climbing up the ladder only to find that the ladder is leaning against the wrong wall.

One of the best ways to cultivate the habit of effectively investing your time is to set a specific time to get out of bed each morning, regardless of how you feel. This early victory of mind over mattress will set the tone for your entire day. Try it for one week. Pick a time and get up at that time every day. Notice how you feel for the rest of the day and how much more you get accomplished when you start the day with a victory like this.

A good way to make sure that you have no trouble scoring your morning victory is to schedule an important task that you enjoy doing for first thing each morning. Normally, this will be one of your "daily half dozen." Not only will it help you get out of bed more easily, you will be able to check off one of your "half dozen" as completed early in the day.

My first task while I was writing this book was to complete my 2000 words of writing. To do it, I forward the phone and shut out all interruptions so that I can concentrate and enjoy my work. On days when it is difficult to crawl out of bed, I invest a few moments in thinking of how much I enjoy writing, of the sense of accomplishment I will have when I finish the book, of how much a difference the book will make in the lives of others, of how it will lead me closer to my Primary Overall Goal, and of how lucky I am to be free to pursue my dream so easily each morning. Suddenly, the comforter seems less comforting, and I roll easily out of bed and into the shower.

- **Reward results, not activity.** You learned earlier that you should set up a series of milestones on the way to your goal and then reward yourself for achieving them. You may also reward yourself each day for completing your "daily half dozen." When you are setting up this goal-achievement awards program for yourself, make sure you are rewarding the right things. Reward results, not activity. **Spending 10 hours one day on your business is worthless unless those 10 hours were spent on goal-achieving activities.** You could spend 10 hours every single day for the next 10 years and never make any progress if you are wasting the 10 hours on shuffling papers, "getting ready" to start projects, making trivial phone calls, and other non-goal-achieving activities. In fact, you would probably achieve your goal much quicker if you only worked two hours a day, but you made sure that those two hours were dedicated solely to high-level goal-achieving activities.

> *Those four principles - only compare yourself to your own benchmarks, be selfish of your time, use the tools of business, and reward results not activity - will give you the basis for a sound goal-achievement scorecard.*

Here's how to put them together to create your ideal tracking system:

• Use a time log to keep you on track to your goals

How many hours a week do you spend doing high-level activities that contribute directly to achieving your Primary Overall Goal? Do you have any idea at all?

Probably not.

And if you guess, I would almost guarantee that your guess is much higher than the actual number.

Why?

We do not realize how much time we waste on trivial activities like getting ready in the morning, taking coffee breaks, calling friends, reading the paper, sorting mail, and other mundane tasks that don't contribute directly to achieving our goals.

If you are going to maximize the speed of your journey toward your goal, you MUST know exactly

where you are investing your time now and where you should be investing your time in the future.

Keeping a daily time log will make this easy. Here's how to do it:

1. Get a sheet of blank paper, preferably graph paper. Across one side of the sheet, list the top priority activities in your life. For example, you may have prospecting, practicing your sales presentation, family time, reading and studying, exercise, and time spent on reviewing and visualizing your goals.

2. Down the other side of the paper, write the dates of the next 21 days. Carry this sheet with you wherever you go during the next 21 days and record the productive time that you actually have during that day. The easiest way to do this is to record how you spend your time in tenths of an hour. For example, if you spend 20 minutes exercising, round it off to three-tenths of an hour and record it as 0.3 in your log. Be sure you only record the time you actually spend exercising, NOT the time you spend traveling to the gym, changing clothes, or getting ready to exercise.

3. Follow this same procedure for all your activities during the next 21 days. Be zealous about it and be honest with yourself. Time spent sorting mail does NOT count as productive work time. Time spent at the water cooler or on coffee breaks does NOT count as prospecting time. Time spent watching TV does NOT count as productive family time.

The average American spends 30 hours per week working, 10 hours at work doing non-work activities such as coffee breaks, 7 hours watching TV, 13 hours in other social

> *activities, and 50 hours in unstructured time and maintenance activities such as eating, showering, and doing errands. Of the 30 hours spent working, only about 8-10 are actually good, solid uninterrupted highly creative hours spent completing goal-achieving activities.*

What you want to do is get an idea of how many hours in a week you are actually doing productive, goal-achieving activities. You will also learn how many hours you are spending in routine, non-goal-achieving activities such as commuting, getting ready for work, chatting with friends, piddling around the house, or running errands. These everyday activities are obviously not the highest and best use of your time and they should be your first targets for delegation.

If you are like most people who do this exercise, you will be shocked at how few productive hours you actually have in a week. And amazed at how those hours add up over the course of the year.

> *If you spend one hour each day getting ready for work and another hour commuting (1/2 hour each way), you have invested 10 hours per week just in getting to work. That adds up to 500 hours per year, or the equivalent of about 12 full work weeks. That is why people always ask me how I get so much done when it seems like I never work. Just by working out of my home office, I have gained 500 hours per year in otherwise wasted time.*

What if you can't work out of a home office?

Your goal with any non-productive activity that you cannot eliminate is to transform it into productive time that will help you achieve your goal.

For example, you could invest those 500 hours in listening to tapes of various personal development, business, or other educational books. By the end of the year, you would have the equivalent of a full year of college education just by listening to tapes each day.

<u>Do not skip this exercise. It is one of the most important ones you can do.</u> Until you really know how you are investing your time now, you will not know what areas you need to refine in order to achieve your goals in a quicker and easier manner.

If you find that you are investing relatively few hours in goal-achieving activities, don't be frustrated.

Rejoice.

If you have accomplished all that you have by investing only a few hours per week in goal-achieving activities, think how much you could accomplish by investing an extra 10-15 hours to move you closer to your goals?

Have faith that there is a divine plan at work and it is unfolding beautifully, even if you don't like all the physical results at the moment. Understand that the results you have today are a product of the thoughts you had yesterday (or last week or last year). You can change your thoughts, so you can change your life.

Begin today to focus your thoughts on the magnificent life of beauty and joy that you are creating. Claim this life for yourself right now in your mind and in your heart. By doing so, you will already be living it on the spiritual and intellectual levels. Then begin today to take actions on a regular basis that move you closer to living this life in physical reality. It will only be a matter of time until your dreams come true.

• **In fulfilling your dream, you're in business for yourself.** Use the tools of business - lists, computers, phone calls, meetings, networking - to turn your dream into a reality sooner. **Treat your goal-achievement process as running your own multi-million dollar corporation. Think as if you are the CEO of your corporation** who is in charge of setting up systems and procedures that make sure you reach your goals in the speediest, easiest, and best manner.

One of the most important systems you can set up is a tracking system to measure your progress toward your goal. You have already created a daily time log, so you now know how you are investing your time in moving closer to your goal. The next step is to create a log so that you will be able to track the results that your investment of time is giving you.

Here is how to do that:

1. Get a clean sheet of paper, preferably graph paper. Write your Primary Overall Goal in bold letters across the top. Then place your date you would like to achieve your goal in bold letters in the upper right hand corner. Under your goal, write, "Reasons why" and then describe in detail all the benefits you will receive from achieving your goal. Then make a box and title it, "Reward," and describe in detail the reward you will give yourself for achieving your goal. For example, if your goal is to earn $1,000,000, your reward might be a trip around the world or a down payment on your dream home.

2. Then create a section titled, "Steps to complete." Fill in the first step that you must take to get you closer to your goal and the date that you will take it. If you have already completed some of the steps toward your goal, fill them in and then place check marks next to them to indicate they are finished. Next to the date column, add a column titled, "Reward," and fill in the smaller rewards that you will give yourself when you complete that step. If you do not know all the steps you will need to take to achieve your goal, great. That means it is a lofty goal and well worthy of stretching to

achieve. Fill in whatever steps you do know. Once you have completed those steps, your increased level of awareness will allow you to see what the next step should be and you can fill that in when you know it.

Now, you have a simple goal-achievement tracking form that will keep you on target to achieving your goals. Review it at least once a day, really concentrating on feeling the emotions associated with achieving your goal and all the benefits and rewards you will receive when you do.

The second tracking form that will be helpful is one to chart the completion of your "daily half dozen." The simplest way to do this is to get a sheet of graph paper and list your daily half dozen down one side. Then put the next 30 days' dates across the other side. You can track your progress one of two ways.

The first option is to just check off the activities that you complete each day. For example, if you completed all six activities on March 10, put check marks by each activity under the March 10 column on your sheet. At the end of 30 days, total up your check marks for each of your six activities. You may have 24 check marks for "Prospecting at least one hour," and 27 check marks for "Spending one hour of quality time with my family." Divide the number of check marks you have into the number of days to get a percentage of the total days that you actually did what you said you would do. In this case, you did your prospecting 80% of the time (24/30) and your family time 90% (27/30) of the time. This is an easy way to track how you are doing and what areas you need to focus on. If you saw, for example, that your sales were not as high as you would like them to be, you could look at your chart and see that you skipped six days of prospecting. This easily explains why you aren't achieving your goal as quickly as you would like and gives you an easy way to re-focus your time.

Stress-Free Success • 219

In the beginning, you may find that a couple of your key areas do not get finished every day. It sometimes takes a while to form the habit of living at 100% every single day. Do not despair. You are competing only against yourself. Keeping a chart like this gives you a benchmark so that you can improve. If you only completed one of your "daily half dozen" 10 times in 30 days, don't get annoyed at yourself for blowing off the other 20 days. Just focus on that activity and improve your total in the next 30 days.

The key is constant improvement. If you accomplished one of your key tasks 15 times last month, go for 25 times this month, and then 30 times next month. If you are continually improving, you will be continually moving toward your goal. You can live your life joyously and without stress because you will know that you are doing the right things at the right time to achieve your goal. You know that it is only a matter of time until you reach your goal.

The second way to set up a chart to keep you on track to achieving your goals is to track the exact activity that you did in each area each day. To do this, set up the top of your chart exactly as you did in the first example. Get a sheet of graph paper and list your daily half dozen down one side. Then put the next 30 days' dates across the other side. Instead of just checking off whether or not you completed the activity, write down how much you did each day. For example, if you invested one hour and ten minutes in prospecting, put "1:10" in the prospecting column. If you ran 5.2 miles, put "5.2" in the exercise mileage column. If you ate 2,450 calories, put "2,450" in the calories column.

At the end of each week and the end of the month, you can add up the totals in each column and see how they compare to your goals. If one of your daily half dozen was to eat less than 2,500 calories per day, you know that in 30 days, you should have consumed less than 75,000 calories. It is easy to look at your total and see how you are doing in relation to your goals.

This **builds in a little leeway for a flexible schedule.** If you know you are going to take a three-day weekend next week, you can run a few extra miles or invest a few extra hours in prospecting this week so that you are ahead of schedule when you take time off. This is how I do my tracking. If I know I will be travelling, I work out a couple extra days before I go so that I can take the weekend off when I'm on the road. Or I write a couple thousand extra words in advance, so I can take a day off and still be on schedule.

Using a daily time log, a goal-achievement steps chart, and a "daily half dozen" tracking chart like this will make it easy for you to keep yourself focused on high-level, goal-achieving activities.

Fine tune your actions

Top competitors at every level know that there is a razor's edge between winning and losing. They focus much of their attention on fine-tuning their skills to give them the edge they need to win the gold. Follow their lead by applying these three principles:
- **Concentrate on flow experiences**
- **Follow a strict daily personal development program**
- **Live in the present but work toward the future**

Flowing toward your goal smoothly

One of the most important things to remember in this whole goal-achievement process is that the climb should be just as enjoyable as the view from the summit. After all, most of your life will be spent in the climb toward your goals so if you don't enjoy the climb, you won't enjoy your life.

Don't worry about results so much that you aren't enjoying the climb toward your goal. In his excellent book, *Flow: The Psychology of Optimal Experience*, Mihaly

Csikszentmihalyi describes this enjoyment of the journey as the experience of "flow." He says:

> "You don't conquer anything except things in yourself... The justification of climbing is climbing, like the act of writing justifies poetry... The purpose of flow is to keep on flowing, not looking for a peak or a utopia, but staying in the flow."

Besides being the key to enjoying life, viewing your activities as potential flow experiences will also help you develop the razor's edge you need to win. If you are enjoying an activity for what it is, without worrying about whether you are doing it right or how fast or how long you are doing it, you will be relaxed. All of your mental and physical muscles will be able to perform optimally. You will free yourself from the mental blocks that hold most of us back. You will glide through life with effortless ease like a figure skater across the ice. And, your potential will be free to flow forth like a stream running into the ocean.

The 7-step formula for enjoying all the activities in your life

According to psychologists, enjoyment does not depend on what you do, but on how you do it. You are free to transform your daily activities into intensely satisfying, flow experiences by applying this process:

1. Set your Primary Overall Goal (POG)
2. Develop milestones along the way to achieving your POG
3. Track your progress toward your goal
4. Concentrate 100% of whatever task you are doing. Be here now, as the Eastern mystics say
5. Make finer and finer distinctions in the level of activities that you are accomplishing
6. Refine your skills to meet the increasing challenges you face
7. Keep raising the stakes every time you achieve one goal or pass one milestone

Following this process will assure you of living a richly rewarding and intensely satisfying life on the path to achieving your goals.

> *As Mihaly Csikszentmihalyi said, "It is when we act freely, for the sake of the action itself rather than for ulterior motives, that we learn to become more than what we were. When we choose a goal and invest ourselves in it to the limits of our concentration, whatever we do will be enjoyable."*

Never forget, as Lao Tzu said, **"The way is the goal."**

- **Follow a daily personal development program**

One of the most critical, and most often overlooked aspects of creating your perfect life is developing a sound education and personal development program. By reading this book AND completing the exercises that it suggests, you have made a major stride in the right direction. Here are some other points to keep in mind when you are putting your program together:

- **Self-improvement precedes self-fulfillment.** This is another area where people confuse the law of cause and effect. Self-improvement is the cause. Self-fulfillment is the effect. Don't try to get the effect without first working on the cause.

- **Balance your production with improving your ability to produce.** Time is the one constant in your life. We all have 24 hours each day, no more, no less. You must invest a portion of this time in improving yourself so that you will become aware of how to produce more, give more, and achieve more in less time. If you do not make this investment and instead spend all of your time in production (work), you are locking yourself in to the same level of production for the rest of your life because you will not be learning and growing.

You will also be missing out on much of the joy in life that comes from learning new skills and developing higher levels of wisdom and understanding.

- **Work as hard on yourself as you do on your job.** Which one is more important- becoming a better person or becoming a better worker? In the long run, becoming a better person will automatically make you better on your job. You will find yourself able to do more with less effort and earn more in less time. Working on yourself is some of the most profitable work you will ever do.

- **Emphasize BE over BUY.** Your self-education is THE BEST long-term investment you will ever make. Investing in yourself will give you fabulous dividends for the rest of your life - not only financial, through increased earnings power, but mental and spiritual, through healthier relationships and a better understanding of yourself and the world around you. Most importantly, regular self-education will assure you that you are continuing to grow; and as you know, we either grow or die; there is no stay the same.

Your very own gold mind

Create your own intellectual, financial, and spiritual feast by setting up a regular program of self-education. Most Americans spend about 6 percent of their income on food and 12 percent on automobile expenses, but almost nothing on self-education. People say they can't afford to buy books or tapes or attend seminars.

That's ridiculous.

Think of it this way:

> *If I came to you and told you that you had an incredible gold mine in your backyard, but it would cost $1,000 for a special shovel that you needed to mine the gold, would you go out and find a way to come up with the $1,000?*

Of course you would.

That's the same way that the gold mind in your head works. It won't just create a few golden nuggets; it can create immense boulders of wealth in your life - IF you will invest in the shovel that you need to develop your mind-mine.

Set aside at least 5 percent of your income to use for improving yourself. Put this money aside first when you receive a paycheck. Set up a plan for how you will invest it. Emphasize be over buy. This means to invest your money in things that will help you become a better person, rather than things that will give you the false appearance of having become a better person. Here are some key areas to include in your personal development program:

- **Books and tapes**

Invest in books on a regular basis. For about the cost of a movie, a book or tape gives you the chance to enter the minds of the world's greatest thinkers. And if cash is tight, you can check out the books and tapes for free at your local library. I would suggest buying as many books as you can, however. Read them actively. Highlight key points that you want to remember. When you are finished with the book, go back and read your highlighted portions to review the book's major ideas. Jot down the most important ideas in a notebook or in a word processing file on your computer.

The average American reads less than one book per year and 58% of Americans never finish a book after high school. Reading regularly will give you an incredible edge over most everyone around you. If you read one book a month for 20 years, you'll have digested the wisdom of 240 books.

Who has the advantage - you, the reader - or your competition, the non-reader?

- **Seminars**

Seminars give you the chance to learn from the greatest minds in the world live. If the seminar is set up in a workshop format, you will also be able to ask questions and receive feedback on your ideas. One of the most beneficial reasons to attend seminars is to meet like-minded people who can help you along the road to your perfect life. The next person you meet at a seminar may become your mentor or success partner. Or they have the key that opens the door to achieving your primary goal quicker and easier than you ever thought possible. When you are deciding which seminars to attend, try to pick a balance of topics and types of speakers. Attend seminars in areas outside your major occupation, such as ones dealing with health, massage, science, or history. This will help you develop a balanced perspective on life and will open your eyes to new ways of thinking and looking at the world.

- **The finer things in life**

Use a portion of your Self-Education Fund to experience the finer things in life. Take dance lessons, attend the opening night of a play, spend an afternoon in an art museum, savor the delicacies in a fine restaurant. Really get into each experience so you learn from it and grow because of it. Study tapes of Fred Astaire and Ginger Rogers or whoever the best dancers are in your field. Learn the history and culture behind the play you are watching. Get a book on basic art history and begin to learn about how the different types of art reflect the culture that they were produced in. Talk to your chef about how he prepares your meal and what spices and other "secrets" give it its fine flavor.

- **Find an expert and ask for help**

Another great way to invest your self-education funds is to take a successful person out to dinner. Most successful people would be flattered if you called and offered to take them to dinner and told them you wanted to learn what made them successful. Use this opportunity to really listen and learn. Ask them how they got started, what they biggest challenges and successes have been, what books they read, who they have learned from, what the most important lessons they've learned along the way are, and what gives them their drive and ambition.

If you did this once a month for a year, how far ahead do you think you would be at the end of the year? What kinds of contacts would you have made? How far would you have progressed toward achieving your goal?

• **Live in the present, but work toward the future**

The final key to fine-tuning your goal-achievement program is to develop the ability to live in the present, while working toward the future. When you have a plan for the future, such as the one you've developed by completing the exercises in this book, you can relax and enjoy the perfection of the present moment, because you know that the future you desire will come in the perfect time in the perfect way.

As the saying goes, **"Be here now."** Really, when you think about it, you can't be anywhere else but here, so enjoy each one of your present moments for what they are.

Know that your life is unfolding according to the perfect plan, which you gave direction to when you developed your goal-achievement program.

Have fun with life.

Make your goal-achieving a "play project," something you look forward to each day.

As the great bard Shakespeare said, **"No profit grows where is no pleasure ta'en."**

Take pleasure in all you've accomplished so far and all you will accomplish in the future.

Stop for a minute and reflect on how far you've come so far. After all, by completing the exercises in this book, you're ahead of 99% of the population already.

Then, turn the page and get ready for the "Final Frontier" on your road to Stress-Free Success.

Lesson 14:
Your Next Step... Work With A SuccessCoach To Keep You On Track To Stress-Free Success

The Final Frontier

Congratulations! You are right on track to be one of the few people in the world who can truly say they are living their dreams and achieving their goals without giving up their lives.

You have only two more steps to go on the road to Stress-Free Success:

1. *Model after other champions*
2. *Work with a SuccessCoach to keep you on track to achieving your goals without giving up your life*

Model after other champions

The next key to managing your team to a Gold Medal is to find other champions and model your team after the behaviors that have worked for them.

As you now know, **inner achievement leads to outer achievement.** Without the inner processes working in harmony, the outer achievement will not occur or will not last. Therefore, look for role models of inner achievement.

- *What inner traits do you admire most?*
- *What inner talents will it take for you to achieve your goal?*
- *Who has these traits and talents?*

- What values do they have that allowed them to develop these traits?
- How can you learn from them?

Don't worry about whether or not you know these people or think you can meet them. You can still learn from them through reading newspaper and magazine articles, checking out their biographies, listening to interviews, talking to other people who know them, and watching how they react to different situations.

As Denis Waitley says, **"When you find a master mind, become a master mime."**

Find people who have overcome your fears and learn from them. Find people who have done what you want to do and model them. Find people who are the kind of person you want to become and get to know them. Find people who have the same kinds of goals and dreams and spend time with them.

That last idea is important.

The company you keep plays a major role in determining the way you look at the world and the actions you take.

> Who do you spend time with now? What are these people doing to you? Is the association moving you closer to your goal or is it keeping you from achieving your goal? Do these people support and encourage you or tear you down? Do they want you to succeed or do they want you to remain mediocre like them? Do they spend time building for the future or re-living the past?

Join a group with the same kinds of goals and dreams, not the same problems.

> If you hang around with a bunch of fat people, it's not likely you'll ever get thin. Your role models will all be fat. You will find yourself talking about overeating and what it's

> like to be fat. Your thoughts will dwell on being fat. You will look in the mirror and see yourself as fat. You will get put down every time you try to quit being fat. You will remain fat.
>
> If you hang around with a bunch of alcoholics, your role models will be alcoholics. You'll think about being an alcoholic. You'll look in the mirror and see yourself as an alcoholic. You will remain an alcoholic.

Hard as it may be, **you MUST quit spending time with people who have the same problems as you do.**

You must also quit spending time with people who do not support your goals and dreams. The balance between mental thoughts and physical reality is too precarious to take a chance on a bunch of nitwits upsetting it. You don't have to make a big deal out of it. Just begin replacing your old associates with new ones who encourage you and uplift you. Soon you will be surrounded by a group of champions just like yourself. And when a pack of champions bursts out of the gate, there's no stopping them on the way to victory.

Do you remember the famous song with the words, "I am a rock. I am an island"?

Despite those lyrics, we are not "rocks" and no human is an "island." We are all connected and even the best of us need the support and encouragement of others in order to stay on track to achieving our goals.

Everyone needs a mentor and a success partner

A mentor is someone who has done what you would like to do. This person can help you avoid the pitfalls along the way and teach you the shortcuts and introduce you to the people who can make your journey even smoother and more enjoyable. When you find someone who you would like to be your mentor, don't be afraid of asking them. Most successful people are flattered that you value their opinion and would be happy to share their ideas with you.

Don't expect your mentor to be perfect in every area. We all have our strengths and weaknesses. It is perfectly acceptable, and in fact I would strongly recommend, to have different mentors for different areas of your life. Pick the best person in each area and then learn from them. That way you're getting the best of the best at all times. The person who is best to mentor you on how to build a billion-dollar corporation may not be the best person to mentor you on how to build a beautiful marriage. That's fine. Just find a different mentor for your love relationships.

A success partner is another key person to build a solid relationship with. A success partner who is someone who shares your love of learning and growing. The two of you will share your goals and commit to helping each other achieve them. This means you will be accountable to each other for taking goal-achieving action daily.

Mike Fry, president of Total Sports Photography and Fancy Fortune Cookies, is my own success partner. While I was writing this book, we called each other early each morning and went over our goals for the day. We kept each other accountable for actually doing every day what we said we were going to do.

If one of us wasn't doing what we needed to, we got on each other's case a bit. We reminded each other of all the great things that we were attracting to us as we achieved our goals. And, when something good happened to us, we were on the phone to share it with each other immediately. This kind of partnership made a huge difference in our success and I strongly recommend you find a success partner to help you turn your dreams into reality.

Even champions have coaches

Think for a minute about top athletes like Michael Jordan, Cal Ripken, Troy Aikman, and others. What comes to your mind?

World-class performance, right?

Now, think for another minute about how they got that way.

The answer is simple: they all have coaches who help them stay focused and on track as well as provide them with the increasingly fine distinctions that separate the champions from the rest of the world.

Why should you be any different?

There's absolutely no reason you shouldn't have a SuccessCoach also - someone who will help you stay on track and someone who will provide YOU with the increasingly fine distinctions that will allow you to lead a world-class life.

That sounds good, you say, but how do I find a coach like that?

I've got the answer for you.

Read on.

Your Next Step

To help you put the ideas in Stress-Free Success into action in your life and to help you stay on track and be accountable for your success, **I've developed a special Mentoring and SuccessCoaching program for you. I'll be working one-on-one with a small group of people who are serious about living the principles of Stress-Free Success.**

We'll focus on getting you perfectly clear about what direction you want to go and what your ideal life looks like, as well as on developing and IMPLEMENTING your Daily Stress-Free Success Action Plan.

Plus, because I'm one of the best direct-response copywriters in the country and ran my own marketing consulting business for years, we're also going to focus on high-impact, low-stress marketing techniques that will put all kinds of extra income on your bottom line.

If you're really serious about achieving your goals without giving up your life, send me a fax to 913-789-8999 and I'll get an application packet out to you for this special program.

And, if you're not sure you're ready to commit to a SuccessCoaching program right now, your next step should be to get a copy of my **Stress-Free Success System Home Study Course**. The course takes all the ideas and principles in this book and expands on them so you'll have an easier time implementing them in your life. It also includes worksheets for all the key exercises as well as audio tapes I produced to highlight the key points of the course and show you how people from around the world are using it successfully.

Once again, if you're interested in finding out more about this course, give me a call or send me a fax to 913-789-8999 and I'll get the information to you immediately.

Now, let's move on to helping you choose your mentors, success partners, and SuccessCoaches.

Write the names of your ideal mentors, success partners, and SuccessCoaches here (even if you currently do not know them- remember, you must provide the *what* and your subconscious will help you with the *how*):

Mentor's Name	Date I'll Contact Them	Phone
1. *Jeff Smith*	*Immediately*	913-789-8803
2. _____	_____	_____
3. _____	_____	_____

Beside each name, write the date that you will contact them to discuss helping you in a mentor-type relationship. Then contact them.

Well, we've now come to a crossroads. You've come to understand yourself better; your level of awareness is up; you've set your goals and have a very clear picture of where you're going; your daily Stress-Free Success Plan is in place; and you've now chosen your mentor, success partner, and SuccessCoach.

Congratulations! You've really come a long way since the start of this book.

Now, all that's left is for you to continue executing your Stress-Free Success Plan and continue working with your SuccessCoach to make ever finer distinctions of what success really means to you.

I look forward to hearing your success stories (please do write and share them with me) and hopefully, to working with you in my SuccessCoaching program and through my Stress-Free Success home study course.

Before I go, I want to leave you with one thought that sums up what this whole process is really about:

"The highest reward for a person's toil is not what they get for it, but what they become by it."

John Ruskin

Best wishes for a richly rewarding, thoroughly enjoyable, marvelously prosperous journey toward your ideal life,

Jeff

To contact the author...

Jeff Smith is available for live programs, individualized SuccessCoaching sessions, and other programs designed to help you or your organization function at a championship level.

To find out more about these programs, please call Jeff at 913-789-8803, fax him a description of what you're looking for to 913-789-8999 or write

Jeff Smith
c/o Center For Personal Excellence
3156 Woodview Ridge, Suite 301-BK
Kansas City, KS 66103

To continue your journey...

To continue your journey toward Stress-Free Success, **please fax this page to me at 913-789-8999** or mail it to me **c/o Center For Personal Excellence, 3156 Woodview Ridge, Suite 301-BK, Kansas City, KS 66103**, so I can get you the information you need to take the next step in your wonderful journey. Thanks,

> ❑ I'd like to receive your Special Report, "Stress-Free Success: Phase Two" (a $10 value) **FREE**. I'm enclosing $3 to cover shipping & handling. (Please MAIL cash or check payable to Center For Personal Excellence to address listed above.)

❑ I'd like to order _____ additional copies of *Stress-Free Success*. I'm enclosing a check made payable to The Center For Personal Excellence in the amount of $12.95 + $2.00 shipping each.

❑ I'd like more information about the Stress-Free Success Home Study Course, Life Management System and other programs.

FREE BONUS ($100 value)
As a special thank you for helping me make *Stress-Free Success* a best-seller, I'm including this $100 bonus for you FREE (check below if you'd like to receive it FREE.)

❑ I understand that as a reader of this book, I can qualify to participate in a Stress-Free **SuccessCoaching** session FREE (a $100 value). Please contact me with details.

❑ I have an individual or organization in mind who may be interested in having you work with them to benefit from the Stress-Free Success Strategies. Please contact me to discuss.

On a scale of 1 to 10 (with 10 being the highest), I'd rate *Stress-Free Success* (circle one):   1   2   3   4   5   6   7   8   9   10

❑ I am providing you with a testimonial about how *Stress-Free Success* influenced my life. (You may attach a separate sheet)
    ❑ Please feel free to use it in future promotions.
    ❑ Please do <u>not</u> use it in future promotions.

Your name _____

Your profession _____ Are you an owner in the business? _____

Your address _____

City, State, ZIP _____

Phone _____   FAX _____

E-Mail (if you have one) _____

(You may attach your business card, if you'd like)